SECURITIES ░ INS
S E R V I C

CU00712558

An Introduction to
FINANCIAL
SPREAD BETTING
Shares and Indices

An Introduction to
FINANCIAL
SPREAD BETTING
Shares and Indices

Jon Eagle SIAff

First edition first published in 2003 in Great Britain by
Securities Institute Services Limited
Centurion House, 24 Monument Street
London EC3R 8AQ, England.

Written by Jon Eagle SIAff

ISBN: 1 84307 069 3
First edition printed May 2003

While every effort has been made to ensure its accuracy, no
responsibility for loss occasioned to any person acting or
refraining from action as a result of any material in this
publication can be accepted by the publisher or author.

Printed and bound in Great Britain by
Antony Rowe Ltd, Wiltshire.

Contents

Acknowledgements

Charts kindly provided by ShareScope - www.sharescope.co.uk, Bloomberg and Updata.

Thanks also to Lewis Findlay, Managing Director, Cantor Index

Other Books By The Author

Also By
Jon Eagle

Fiction Novels
Red
(ISBN 1-85863-841-0)

Essex Boys
(ISBN 0-9537466-7-4)

About the Author

Jon Eagle has worked in the UK financial markets since the 1980's and qualified as a Registered Representative of The Securities Association whilst working for Lloyds Bank Financial Services.

In 2000, he joined Cofunds, the independent fundmarket, as a founder member of their operations team.

Chapter 1

WHY USE A FINANCIAL BOOKMAKER?

1.1 Introduction

Today is an age of unlimited opportunity, an era of outstanding new ideas, emerging industries and new frontiers. There are huge developments in technology, medicine, computer software, military capabilities and innovative new companies.

Over the long term stock markets will continue to grow. Entrepreneurial, dynamic businesses developing new products, new services and innovative technologies are likely to drive the markets upwards. History shows that stock markets rise and reach record levels time after time, despite recessions, corrections, crashes and major bear markets such as those experienced in the past few years.

For the financial spread bet trader, stock market falls simply present another opportunity to make money (as well as the risk of losing some). Via the internet, individuals have more access to more information than ever before. Today's ever advancing technology makes spread betting accessible to a wider audience than was ever previously imagine.

> *"Far better it is to dare mighty things, to win glorious triumphs, even though checkered by failure, than to rank with those poor spirits who neither enjoy much nor suffer much, for they live in the gray twilight that knows not victory, nor defeat."*
>
> Theodore Roosevelt

1.2 Join The Club

The world of financial spread betting can be an exciting and profitable one - but this is no longer an exclusive club. Anyone, even with the most limited resources, can open an account with a financial bookmaker and trade just like the 'big boys'.

This book will give you all the information you need to know to get you started and guide you to success with a step-by-step approach, in an easy to understand, jargon free manner.

1.3 Financial Spread Betting Is Speculative

First of all, make no mistake - financial spread betting is speculative. Whilst it is possible to make large profits, the potential for loss is also great. The purpose of this book is to give you an honest view of the subject and ultimately guide you to success. It will do this by providing all the information you need to understand the basics, pointing out essential strategies to protect your winning trades and to guard against loses.

1.4 The Odds

Anyone new to financial spread betting faces a daunting prospect. It is estimated that 92% of traders lose, just 8% make a profit. The aim of this book is to allow you to join the winners.

1.5 Deposit Accounts

Most financial bookmakers will allow an account to be opened for as little as £250. A more typical amount, however, is likely to be between £1000 and £3000.

1.6 Tax Free Profits

All profits are completely free of tax, both capital gains tax and income tax. This is because HM Customs and Excise accept that all transactions with a financial bookmaker are bets and liable to betting duty. This is paid by the bookmaker and levied on their profits.

However, an individual making a living from the proceeds would be liable for income tax if this was considered their sole source of income.

1.7 No Commission or Fees

Unlike trading through a stockbroker, you pay no commission or stamp duty. So whilst a bet mimics the action of buying and selling a share, you are not actually dealing in the underlying share. As a result there is no stamp duty to pay. The bookmaker makes money via the market spread, which is the difference between the buy and sell price of your bet.

1.8 Buyers and Sellers Welcome

A financial bookmaker will always quote a two-way price. So it's just as easy to sell short (ie, you think the market/your share is going down) as it is to go long (ie, you buy as you think the market/your share is going up).

1.9 Controlled Risk Betting

This is a feature that bookmakers offer that is strongly recommended to all those who are new to financial spread betting. It is a 'safety net' that makes the whole process of financial spread betting far less dangerous. A controlled risk bet has a guaranteed stop loss order attached to it so that if the bookmaker's quote reaches a certain level (chosen by you) your bet will automatically be closed out, including overnight. You will pay a small premium via an increase in the bookmaker's dealing spread for this style of bet but its value cannot be over emphasised. It means that you will always know exactly the maximum amount you can lose on the bet.

For Example:

It is October and you think the FTSE Future is going up. You decide to open a £10 Up Bet on the FTSE December. You open the bet at 4500 and set your guaranteed stop loss at 4400 (100 points below your bet). This means that for every 1 point the index goes up above 4500 you make £10 but if things go wrong, the most you can lose is 100 points × £10 = £1000.

Scenario 1:

Over the next couple of weeks markets across the globe rocket and by the end of October the FTSE December is 5200. You close your position with a profit of 5200 - 4500 = 700 points X £10 = £7000

Scenario 2:

Overnight the market in the Far East collapses and by the following day the FTSE December opens significantly lower at 4100. Your controlled risk bet has automatically closed your bet at 4400 (your stop loss) meaning you have lost 4500 - 4400 = 100 points × £10 = £1000. However without the guaranteed stop loss you will have lost 4500 - 4100 = 400 points × £10 = £4000.

Controlled risk betting is the sensible way to financial spread bet and will guarantee that you always know exactly how much you are risking. Before bookmakers offered stop loss facilities punters were able - and did - lose huge amounts. In 1987 a punter lost over £¾ million to a financial bookmaker when the market dropped 500 points on Black Monday. With the advent of controlled risk betting there is absolutely no need to be exposed to the potential for such huge loses.

1.10 Bet Outside Normal Working Hours

You can bet on a market even when the official market is closed. Most of the financial bookmakers open 24 hours a day from Sunday night until Friday night.

1.11 Bet Online

You can bet real time on the internet with live prices and up to the minute financial news.

1.12 Leverage

Financial betting gives you the ability to be highly leveraged. If you wanted to buy 1000 Royal Bank of Scotland shares at their current price (£15 approx) you would need £15000. If you wanted to bet on the equivalent of 1000 Royal Bank of Scotland shares with a financial bookmaker you would be making a £10 a point bet. You could do this with no up front capital with a credit account or with £1000 of deposit. Any profit would be the same but the difference required in capital is considerable.

1.13 Hedging

Whilst most financial spread bet accounts are used to bet, they can also used for hedging purposes.

For example:

You have a reasonably large portfolio of blue chip UK shares and you think that over the next few months the stock market is going to fall. You could go to your stockbroker and sell all your shares and then buy them back when you think they are on the way up again. This though, would involve considerable cost. You would have the broker's commission to pay, the spread and possibly a capital tax liability. All in all the cost of selling your portfolio and buying it back again will cost you between 7-8% of the total value.

As an alternative you could hedge against the fall in the market by placing a down bet on the FTSE 100 index. Your portfolio would remain intact but any fall in it's value would be covered by your financial spread bet.

1.14 21ˢᵗ Century Technology

As an individual wishing to bet on the financial markets, you really have never had it so good. With access to the countless sources of information via the internet, teletext and business channels on satellite TV you are able to do just about anything a major city financial company could do. Regardless of your background, your nationality, whether you are a man or woman, young or old, today's technology provides a true level playing field and you can bet from anywhere in the world.

1.15 Opening An Account

The process of actually opening account is much the same for all financial bookmakers. You will be asked to complete an application with your personal and banking details. You will also be required to provide proof of identity (your passport) and proof of address (usually an original utility bill).

Where you are applying for credit facilities the bookmaker will also request information relating to your financial status. You will be expected to provide proof of funds by way of share certificates, bank statement and other evidence of investment.

Once accepted, you will be given an account number. If you have chosen the deposit account option you will then need to send a cheque or make a bank transfer to open your account. When cleared, you will be ready to bet.

Any original documentation sent to the bookmaker will be returned, usually be recorded delivery. The bookmaker will also send you a handbook with information about the indices/shares you can bet on and dates contracts trade in and expire.

The main financial bookmakers are:

Cantor Index
One America Square
London EC3N 2LS
Tel: 020 7894 8800
www.cantorindex.co.uk

City Index Limited
16 Finsbury Circus
London EC2M 7PQ
Tel: 020 7550 8500
www.cityindex.co.uk

CMC Spreadbet PLC
66 Prescot Street
London
E1 8HG
Tel: 08000 933633
www.deal4free.com

Financial Spreads (part of IFX Markets Limited)
One America Square
17 Crosswall
London
EC3N 2LB
Tel: 08000 969620
www.finspreads.com

IG Index Plc
Friars House
157 - 168 Blackfriars Road
London
SE1 8EZ
Tel: 020 7896 0011
www.igindex.co.uk

Spreadex Limited
Freepost ANG 7156
PO Box 4116
Dunstable
LU6 1YT
Tel: 01582 538000
www.spreadex.com

All companies listed here are regulated by the Financial Services
Authority.

Chapter 2

BETTING ON FINANCIAL INDICES

2.1 What Is An Index?

A financial index consists of a number of shares in a given market. For example, in London, the FTSE 100 Index consists of the leading 100 shares traded on the London Stock Exchange and in the US the Dow Jones Industrial Average consists of 30 shares. So by betting on an index you are effectively betting on the market as a whole.

Trading on financial indices has long been a favourite bet with the financial bookmakers. Although just about every major index throughout the world can be traded, most bets are placed on the Dow Jones Industrial Average (US Index) and the FTSE 100 index (London).

2.2 FTSE 100

Of the 2,500 + listings on the London Stock Exchange, there are 100 top UK shares which account for around two-thirds of the total business of the exchange. These are the most powerful and actively traded shares. Each of these 100 blue-chip shares are worth a market capitalisation value in excess of £1 billion.

Let's say for example you think that the UK stock market is going to go up. You could bet on a number of the shares within the FTSE 100 index such as BT, Lloyds TSB, Sainsbury, and Vodafone . However to get a true indication of the whole market you would have to place a bet on all 100 stocks which would be impractical. So instead you would place an UP BET on FTSE 100 index.

Your bet will move up or down depending on the price movement of the underlying shares in the FTSE. So if 85 of the FTSE 100 shares are up, the market will be up and consequently your bet will be up.

Here's an example of the FTSE 100 as it appears on the BBC Ceefax service (page 200). As you can see the FTSE 100 is down by 44.9 points. Of the 100 shares in the index 68 are losers (down in price) and 31 are winners (up in price). This total must always add up to 100 so the remaining 1 company's share price must be unchanged.

FTSE-100 at 1508 Winners 31 Losers 68			
FTSE	4389.8	-44.9	at CLOSE
TechMARK100	818.30	+1.97	at CLOSE
Dow Jones	8762.61	-110.35	at 17.00
NASDAQ	1362.61	-18.01	at 17.00
Nikkei	10067.74	+200.29	
Oil $27.05 + 0.03		Gold $306.45 Cls	

2.3 An Example Of A Bet On A FTSE Future

All bets have an expiry date. For the FTSE 100 Future the contract months are March, June, September and December and bets expire on close of business on the 3rd Friday of those months.

Also for the Dow Jones Index Future the contract months are March, June, September and December. Again, they expire on the 3rd Friday of the contract month, so for March it would be at the close of business on the 3rd Friday in March.

Example:

It is October and you think the UK market is going up and that the FTSE 100 index will finish higher by the end of the year. You telephone your bookmaker and ask for a price for the December FTSE Future and are quoted 4090 - 4100. This means that if you want to place a down bet you will be betting the FTSE 100 goes lower than 4090 and if you want to place an up bet you will be betting the FTSE 100 goes higher than 4100.

So you place an up bet of £10 a point. In other words, you are buying £10 on the December FTSE at 4100. By the end of November, you are proved correct and the FTSE has shot up significantly. You decide to close your bet and take the profit. You telephone your bookmaker and ask for a price for the December FTSE Future and are quoted 4700 - 4710. This time, of course, you are selling to close your bet so you are selling £10 at 4700 (the first price quoted).

In this example your profit will be:

4700 - 4100 = 600 points X £10 = £6,000.

2.4 Daily FTSE 100

As well as placing bets on FTSE Future Contracts (expiring in the contract months of March, June, September, December) you can also bet on the Daily FTSE. As the term suggests the market is quoted for a given day, the official market opening times are 8.00am to 4.30pm.

For Example:
You telephone your bookmaker at 10.00am and ask for a price on the Daily FTSE 100. The bookmaker quotes 4450 - 4460. This means if you want to sell (place a down bet) you get 4450 and if you want to buy (place and up bet) you get 4460.

You think the market is going up this afternoon, as you expect Wall Street to open higher (which usually boosts the UK market) so you buy £20 at 4460. This means you make £20 every time the market goes up 1 point.

By 3.30pm that afternoon the UK market is up as a result of Wall Street opening higher. You telephone your bookmaker and ask for a price on the Daily FTSE 100. You are quoted 4600 - 4610. You decide to close your bet and take your profit, so you sell £20 at 4600 (closing your bet).

Result of your bet:

You bought (up bet) £20 at 4460

You sold (down bet) £20 at 4600

4600 - 4460 = 140 X £20 = £2800.

You could also have allowed your bet to expire. It would have been closed automatically at 4.30pm (when the market closed) and your bet would have been closed at the exact closing price of the FTSE 100. No spread is payable.

Please remember with a Daily FTSE bet you obviously need to be correct almost immediately to make a profit as the contract expires very quickly. Some financial bookmakers are also now offering weekly contracts which gives you a little more time. However, until you have gained some experience it is probably advisable to consider the far dated contracts. At least with these, you have more time and do not have to be right straight away.

2.5 Guaranteed Stop Losses And Normal Stop Orders

It is worth mentioning that there are actually two types of stop orders.

A guaranteed stop loss order is charged for. A few points are added to the price you pay. For this, you get exactly what the name implies - a 'guaranteed' stop at a price you have stated.

A normal stop order is placed with the bookmaker at the time of your bet and is free. The bookmaker will register your stop and do their best to close your bet at the price given. However, this is not guaranteed. There are times when shares and indices move very fast and in these circumstances your bet may be closed at a higher or lower price to your stop.

For Example:
You have placed an up bet on the December FTSE Future. The FTSE is currently trading at 4600 and you have placed a stop at 4500. A news story breaks suddenly sending the market down and the next trade is at 4485. Your bet could not traded at 4500 and instead is filled (closed) at 4485. With a guaranteed stop loss the bet would have been closed at 4500. This is why you pay an extra few points.

2.6 Limit Orders

Limit orders allow you to place an order with a financial bookmaker without having to be stuck to a screen all day. Let's say for example you think the UK market is going down and you would like to place a down bet on the September FTSE Future. However you have decided you don't want to place your bet until the September FTSE Future has fallen through 4500. You telephone your bookmaker who tells you the current price is 4520 - 4530. You can now ask to place a limit order to sell £20 a point of September FTSE at 4500. Your order will now be executed if, and when, the price of 4500 is reached. You would also tell the bookmaker good til cancelled (meaning that you wished the order to be executed at the given price until you subsequently told the bookmaker otherwise).

Chapter 3

BETTING ON INDIVIDUAL SHARES

3.1 The Choices

All financial bookmakers offer the facility to bet on individual UK shares. This gives you the opportunity to bet up or down on any FTSE 100 or FTSE 250 share. This gives you 350 of the top UK companies to bet on. Some bookmakers will also quote prices for companies outside the FTSE 350 but this depends on the individual company's liquidity. It is worth bearing in mind though, that smaller companies have larger spreads (the difference between the buy and sell price). In addition, you can also bet on US shares including all 30 in the Dow Jones Industrial Average. Some bookmakers also quote the S&P 500 and the Nasdaq 100 shares. And if all these weren't enough, you can also bet on some European shares.

3.2 Tax Free

As with other bets no income or capital gains tax is payable. This aspect alone clearly presents a significant advantage over actually buying shares.

3.3 The Ability To Sell Short

Most UK stockbrokers will not allow customers to sell short ie, sell shares they do not own in the hope that they can buy them back at a lower price in the future. This means that when dealing with a stockbroker you can only take views on (and buy) shares that you hope will go up. With a financial bookmaker you can bet that a company's shares will go down as well as up.

3.4 An Example Of An Up Bet

Let's take another look at placing an up bet, this time on a UK share.

You have decided that the Banking sector looks strong and have identified Barclays Bank as one that you think will go up. Like with indices, share prices are quoted on a cycle by financial bookmakers that is March, June, September and December.

Let's say it is October, so you will have the opportunity of placing a bet for one of the next two contract months, in this case December and March. You decided to go for the longer dated contract and ask for a price for the March Barclays Bank. You are quoted.

460 - 470. You place an up bet (or buy or buy to open - these terms mean the same) of £50 at 470.

Remember, you want an emergency exit should your bet go wrong, so you need to place a stop. You decide that the most you are willing to risk is £1000 so you ask your bookmaker to place a stop at 450. With this stop in place the maximum you can lose is:

470 - 450 = 20 points X £50 = £1000.

Your bookmaker reads the bet back to you with the stop and asks you to confirm that the stop is good til cancelled. You acknowledge this. Your bet is now up and running.

You are proved correct. By December, Barclays Bank shares have shot up in price. You telephone your bookmaker who quotes 610 - 620.

This means that if you close the bet your profit will be:

610 - 470 = 140 X £50 = £7000.

However you feel that the share is going to rise still further so leave the bet running.

Right again. By the end of January, the shares are still moving up. You telephone your bookmaker and ask for a price for the March Barclays Bank. You are quoted 690 - 700.

This means if you close the bet your profit will be:

690 - 470 = 220 points X £50 = 11000

Again, you leave the bet running, thinking that the price will rise still further.

By mid February, the share price has fallen back a little.

You call your bookmaker who quotes 630 - 640. You decide to close the bet. You sell (down bet, sell to close) £50 at 630.

The result of your bet is:

You bought £50 at 470

You sold £50 at 630

630 - 470 = 160 X £50 = £8000.

3.5 Trailing Stops To Lock In Profit

The importance of stops to provide an emergency exit should a bet go wrong have already been covered. Now I will show you how stops can be used to lock in profit. Again, this is a vital aspect of spread betting you must adopt if you are going to be a winner.

Using the last example, you will see that £3000 of profit was lost when the price of Barclays Bank shares fell between January and mid February. Let's go through the example again this time using trailing stops.

It is October. You telephone your bookmaker and ask for a price for the March Barclays Bank. You are quoted 460 - 470. You place an up bet of £50 at 470.

Remember, you want an emergency exit should your bet go wrong, so you need to place a stop. You decide that the most you are willing to risk is £1000 so you ask your bookmaker to place a stop at 450. With this stop in place the maximum you can lose is:

470 - 450 = 20 points X £50 = £1000.

Your bookmaker reads the bet back to you with the stop and asks you to confirm that the stop is good til cancelled. You acknowledge this. Your bet is now up and running.

You are proved correct. By December, Barclays Bank shares have shot up in price. You telephone your bookmaker who quotes 610 - 620.

This means that if you close the bet your profit will be:

610 - 470 = 140 X £50 = £7000.

You feel that the share is going to rise still further so leave the bet running

However in order to lock in profit you have already made you ask your bookmaker to move your stop from 450 to 600.

This means that should the price suddenly fall, your bet will be closed out at 600. This means your profit will be:

600 - 470 = 130 X £50 = £6500.

By the end of January, the shares are still moving up. You telephone your bookmaker and ask for a price for the March Barclays Bank. You are quoted 690 - 700.

This means if you close the bet your profit will be:

690 - 470 = 220 points X £50 = 11000

Again, you leave the bet running, thinking that the price will rise still further.

You ask your bookmaker to move your stop from 600 to 680.

By mid February, the share price has fallen back a little and is quoted at 630 - 640.

Your bet though, was closed when the price hit your stop of 680.

This means your profit from the bet is:

You bought £50 at 470

Your bet was closed at 630 (£50)

680 - 470 = 210 X £50 = £10,500.

So by trailing a stop loss you have made £10,500 rather than £8,000 in the previous example. Trailing stops is a simple but very important betting strategy.

3.6 An Example Of A Down Bet

It's July 2000 and you have decided that the technology sector is showing signs of weakness. You think that Bookham Technology PLC shares have hit their peak and are likely to fall in price. You telephone your bookmaker asking him to quote the December Bookham Technology. Again, this is a far dated contract as you could have asked for the September Bookham Technology (remember the contract months are March, June, September and December).

You are quoted 4950 - 5000. You are going to place a down bet, go short, sell, sell to open - these all mean the same. Your down bet will be at the lower of the two prices quoted so lets say you place it at £10 at 4950. Like with an up bet you will want an emergency exit should the bet go against you so you will need to place a stop. You decided the most you are willing to risk is £1000 so you place your stop at 5050.

ie, 5050 - 5950 = 100 points X £10 = £1000.

Your bookmaker reads your bet back to you stating that you have sold £10 December Bookham Technology at 4950 with a stop at 5050 and asks you to confirm that the stop is good til cancelled. You agree, your bet is placed.

By September Bookham Technology shares have fallen and you telephone your bookmaker for a price. You are quoted 4050 - 4100. You are tempted to close the bet,

ie, buy to close £10 at 4100 giving you a profit of:

4950 - 4100 = 850 points X £10 = £8500

but think it may have still further to fall so instead you ask to move your stop to 4150, locking in £7000 of profit guaranteed.

4950 - 4150 = 700 points X £10 = £7000.

You let the bet run until the end of November when the price is 1100 - 1150. This time you ask your bookmaker to buy to close £10 of December Bookham Technology PLC at 1150.

BETTING ON INDIVIDUAL SHARES

Your profit on the bet is:

4950 - 1150 = 3800 points X £10 = £38000.

To show you how this bet could have been placed please see the chart below showing the dramatic fall in price of Bookham Technology PLC shares between July 2000 and November 2000 when the 'dotcom boom' turned to bust.

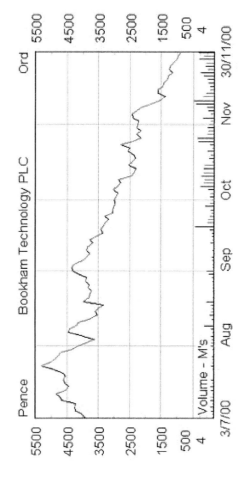

Source: *ShareScope*

Chapter 4

FUNDAMENTAL ANALYSIS

4.1 Different Types Of Analysis

The first three chapters have covered the mechanics of actually placing a financial spread bet and the numerous opportunities there are to bet up or down on different shares and indices. This chapter looks at important rules and strategies that are going to increase your chances of success.

It makes no difference which shares or index you are going to bet on, you have two basic ways to analyse and research. There is fundamental analysis - the study of a company's financial statements in order to measure the value of a company's share price. This study is conducted alongside an analysis of the company's industry in general and the overall economic conditions.

Technical analysis is basically the study of prices. Charts are used to study price movement. You will find that many investors in shares and spread bet punters will fall into one distinct category - they will either stick rigidly to fundamental or technical analysis. There is no need to do so. Why join one camp when you can be in both?

Fundamental analysis can be broken down into three basic areas.

4.2 Economic Analysis

The overall state of the economy is an important element in determining whether conditions are favourable for the stock market. Factors to be considered would include:

- Inflation;
- Retail Price Index;
- Interest Rates;
- Money Supply;
- Gross Domestic Product;
- Balance of Payments;
- The Exchange Rate;
- Retail Sales;
- Government Borrowing.

4.3 Inflation

Inflation is best defined as rising prices. In recent year the UK has experienced relatively low inflation and this has come to be regarded as the norm. However until the mid 1980's the UK had been particularly prone to inflation, regularly having higher inflation than many other major industrialised countries. Amongst the problems caused by inflation are:

- Uncertainty - No one knows what savings will be worth.
- Inequalities - Poorer people are unable to raise their incomes to keep up with inflation. People's buying power decreases.
- Loss of International Competitiveness - When goods are priced higher, foreigners are less likely to buy them.

4.4 Retail Price Index

Retail Price Index (RPI) shows the movement in inflation. It attempts to measure the value of a basket of goods which represents typical family spending. It includes a wide range of items from supermarket products to mortgage costs. Some economists believe that RPI is an unfair measure of inflation because it includes mortgage rates and can be influenced by government policy on interest rates. Instead they monitor the underlying rate of inflation which excludes mortgage rates and concentrates on prices of goods and services. This rate is known as RPIX and is also published by the government. Increases would normally be viewed unfavourably.

4.5 Interest Rates

Interest is the cost of money and its rate could be established by market forces. The government use it as a device to influence economic activity and therefore dictate the level. Interest rates are set by the Monetary Policy Committee of the Bank of England which is given inflation targets set by the government. For example, if the MPC considered that spending levels were too high (inflationary) it would raise interest rates. This would make borrowing more expensive (particularly mortgage payments) and reduce spending and increase saving.

4.6 Money Supply

Money supply is the amount of money in circulation. There are various ways of measuring this, most of which are designated with the letter M as a prefix.

- M0 - refers to the notes and coins ibn circulation and in banks' tills. This is known as narrow money.
- M4 - includes deposits in bank and building society accounts. This is known as broad money.

Growth in money supply is generally viewed as being inflationary.

4.7 Gross Domestic Product

The total value of all goods and services produced by a country is known as its Gross Domestic Product (GDP). This is calculated over a certain period (usually a year) and gives a measure of the overall economic activity within a country. As such a country's GDP is regarded as a measurement of its general wealth. If GDP increases from quarter to quarter the economy is considered to be expanding whereas if GDP decreases from quarter to quarter it is considered to be contracting. If a country's GDP decreases for two consecutive quarters it may be thought to be in recession.

Companies are dependant on the overall economic performance of the country for their own performance. If the economy is growing so should a companies' profits.

Poor economic growth or recession has a detrimental effect on companies' profits and growth.

The annual increase in GDP is often used as a measurement of economic growth.

4.8 Balance Of Payments

The balance of payments is a record of a country's transactions with the rest of the world. This includes trade in manufactured goods, raw materials and services and capital investment. A healthy balance of payments is required for a healthy economy.

4.9 The Exchange Rate

Daily fluctuations in the exchange rate of sterling against other currencies are expected but if the exchange rate becomes higher or lower than its normal range then it will have adverse effects on the economy.

If the exchange rate becomes too high, exporting companies will suffer because their goods will become expensive to foreign buyers. The result will be a reduction in sales or a reduction in prices to keep the sales. Profits will fall either way. Also imports become cheaper which will have a detrimental effect on UK manufacturers who have to cut their prices to compete.

4.10 Retail Sales

Government statistics and statistics produced by retail stores provide an ongoing measure of the economic activities in the high streets. Good sales are important although excessive growth can cause inflationary fears.

4.11 Government Borrowing

The government raises income through taxes. When the government's expenditure exceeds the tax revenues the shortfall is borrowed by issuing bonds. Controlled government borrowing is considered a welcome aspect of the markets as bonds provide a secure investment for investors.

Investors can become concerned when government borrowing increases. Interest rates will have to go up to attract additional funds and the increased government spending will have an inflationary effect.

4.12 Industry Analysis

A company's prospects are influenced considerably by its industry in general. The very best companies can struggle if they are in an industry that is performing poorly. Many believe that a weak company in a strong industry will perform better that a strong company in a weak industry.

4.13 Company Analysis

After studying the economic and industry conditions, the company itself is analysed. The company's financial statements will be scrutinised to gage the company's health.

There are many ways to interpret the information contained in a company's financial statements. The following are covered in this book:

- Earnings Per Share;
- Price Earning Ratio;
- Dividend Yield.

4.14 Earnings Per Share

One of the most important factors an investor will look for is how much income is being earned to assess the potential for growth. Earnings per share shows the amount of profit earned by a company for each ordinary share. This can be defined as:

$$\frac{\text{Profits after tax}}{\text{Number of ordinary shares}}$$

So, for example, if a company has profits of £8.8m after tax and 100m ordinary shares, the calculation is as follows:

$$\frac{\text{Profits after tax (£8.8m)}}{\text{100m ordinary shares}}$$

$$= \frac{£8.8m}{100m}$$

$$= 8.8p$$

Earning per share (EPS) is the profit available to the ordinary shareholders after the deduction of all costs and taxes. It represents the maximum amount that could be paid out as a dividend from the year's profits.

Investors like to see the earning per share of a company increase each year. This enables a company to pay a higher dividend which contributes to growth in the share price. Thus, earning per share growth provides both income and capital growth for the shareholder.

4.15 Price Earnings Ratio

The price earning ratio is defined as:

$$\frac{\text{Price per share}}{\text{Earning per share}}$$

So, if taking the last example, the price per share of the company was 220p the calculation would be as follows:

$$\frac{\text{Price per share (220p)}}{\text{Earnings per share (8.8p)}}$$

$$= \frac{220p}{8.8p}$$

$$= 25p$$

A high price earning ratio (PE) means that there is demand for the shares, most probably because investors are expecting growth. Alternatively, a high price earning ratio could indicate that the shares are overvalued. An investor can compare price earning ratios of different companies and come to a decision as to whether a high PE is justified.

A low PE could mean that a company has limited growth prospects or that the shares are undervalued.

4.16 Dividend Yield

A company making profits will usually pay a dividend to its shareholders, although it is under no obligation to do so. The amount of the dividend is usually expressed as a proportion of the share price, to provide the dividend yield.

The dividend yield can be defined as:

$$\frac{\text{Dividend per share}}{\text{Market price per share}} \times 100\%$$

So, for example if a company has a dividend per share of 6.6p and a share price of 200p the calculation would be as follows:

$$\frac{\text{Dividend per share (6.6p)}}{\text{Market price per share (200p)}} \times 100\%$$

$$= \frac{6.6\text{p}}{200\text{p}} \times 100\%$$

$$= 3.3\%$$

When analysing a company the investor must consider all factors. A company might have a high dividend yield because it has only limited growth prospects. On the other hand, the company could be in difficulty, resulting in a lower share price.

A low dividend yield can indicate that a company has good growth potential. Alternatively it could mean the shares are overvalued.

Chapter 5

TECHNICAL ANALYSIS

5.1 Introduction

Technical analysis, in its simplest form, is the study of prices. This style of analysis dates back over 100 years when Charles Dow recorded his findings, producing the Dow Theory. (His name lives on today, as one half of the Dow Jones Industrial Average. He founded the Wall Street Journal with his partner Edward Jones).

Part of his research brought to light the trending nature of prices and charts were used to record the information. Today, of course, a computer can process the data to create a chart in a matter of seconds.

5.2 Trends

Trends are created by the movement of share prices. When prices are rising, a chart will produce a series of higher tops and higher bottoms and an upward trend is established. When prices are falling, a series of lower tops and lower bottoms will produce a downward trend.

5.3 Using Trendlines

Trends can be identified and measured by the use of 'trendlines'. A trendline is a line drawn between two or more points on a chart. Upward trends are shown by a trendline that is drawn between two or more troughs (low points) and identifies price support. Downward trends are shown by a trendline that is drawn between two or more peaks (high points) to identify price resistance.

Trendlines have been drawn on the chart below for Lloyds TSB Group PLC. From March to September 1997 the shares rise with a series of higher tops and higher bottoms, an upward trend. From October through to November there is some retracement when the shares pull back into downward trend. The shares resume their upward trend in December 1997 moving to over £10 by April 1998.

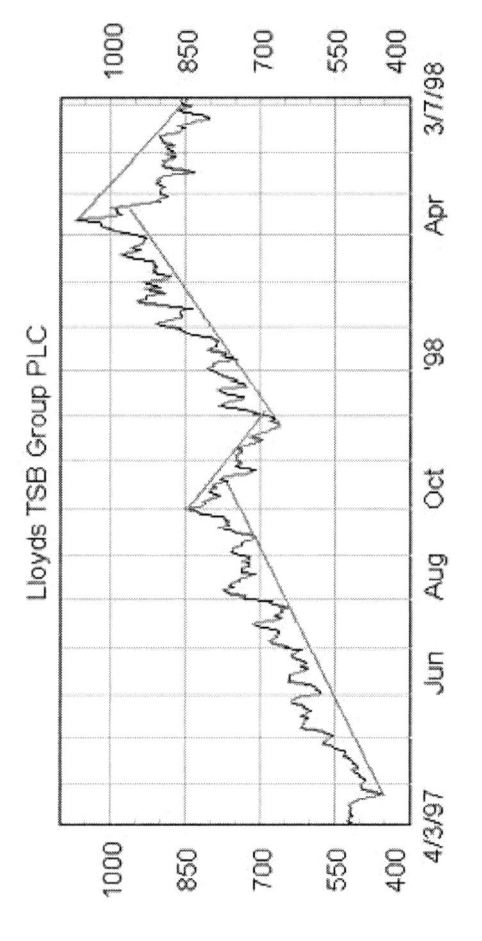

The overall trend for this period is clearly upwards.

Source: *ShareScope*

The chart below shows the share price of Marconi PLC. An uptrend was established from March 2000 with the shares reaching over £12 before their dramatic fall.

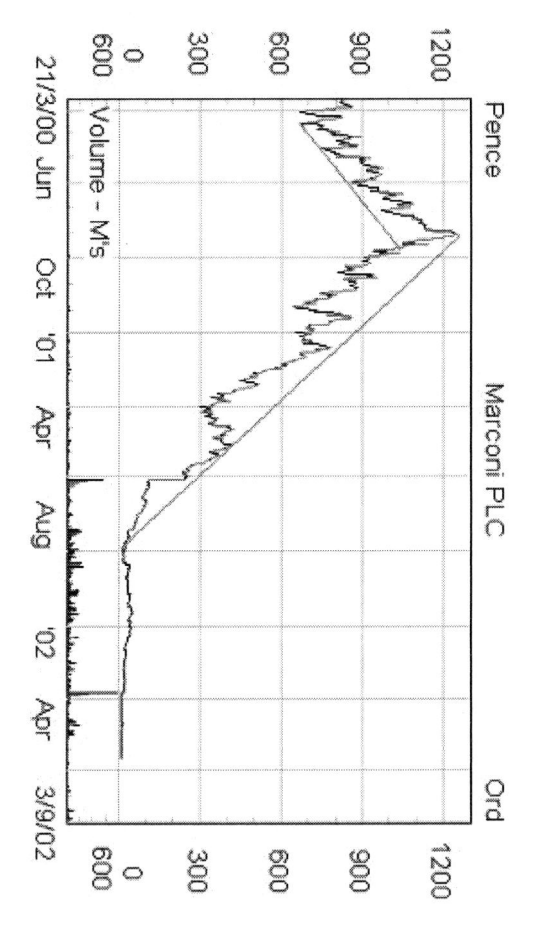

Source: *ShareScope*

5.4 Volume Confirms the Trend

Volume (the amount of shares being traded) should confirm the trend. If the trend is up, volume should increase as the share rises. Similarly if the trend is down, volume should also increase confirming a fall in the share price.

5.5 Reversing of the Trend

A principle of using trendlines is that once a trend has been formed (the trendline has joined two or more troughs for an upward trend or two or more peaks for a downward trend) the trend remains intact until broken, giving a signal that the current trend has reversed.

On the face of it, this may sound very simple but the key to success is to study the current trend using trendlines and then either follow the current trend or wait for the trendline to be broken and then follow the new (reversed) trend.

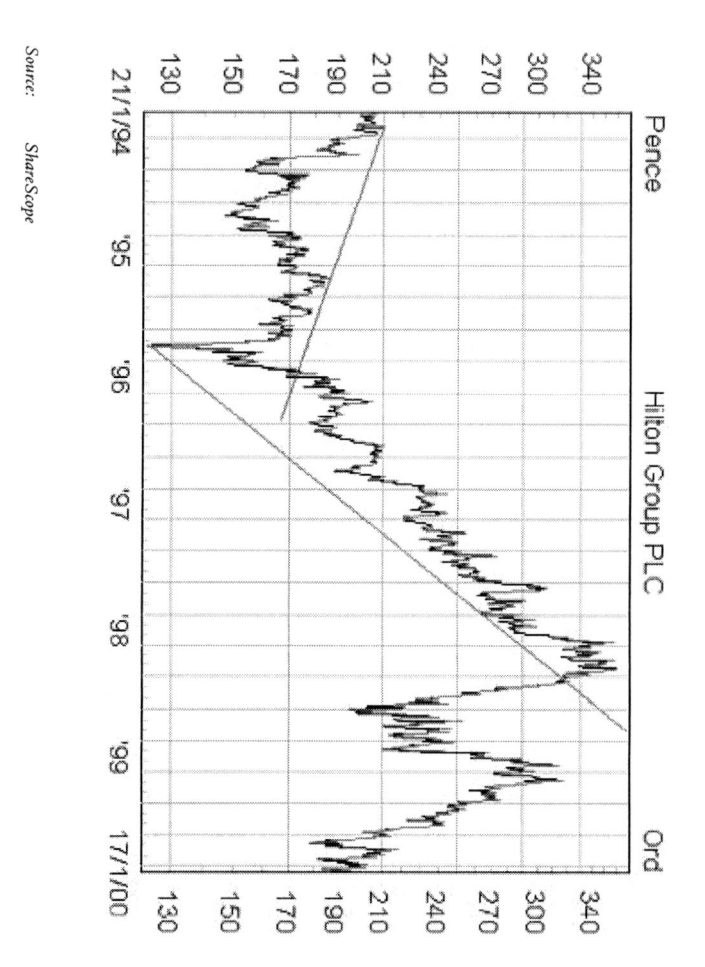

Source: ShareScope

Take a look at the chart above for the hotel chain Hilton Group PLC. Here you will see that the first trendline drawn on the chart is for a downward trend. The share price hits a low point towards the end of 1995 before reversing. The downward trendline has been extended to show a break in the trendline in

January1996 at 174p. As you can see the shares then trend upwards until 1998 hitting a peak of 360p in June 1998 before falling. Again, the upward trendline is extended. A trend reversal is indicated when the trendline is broken in July1998 and the shares drop below 317p.

Take a look at another fine example of the trendline as an indicator. The chart below shows the FTSE 100 from 1994 to 2002. The trendline shows an upward trend which is broken at the beginning of 2001 at around the 6000 mark. This was clearly a good time to sell, the market having fallen to below 4000.

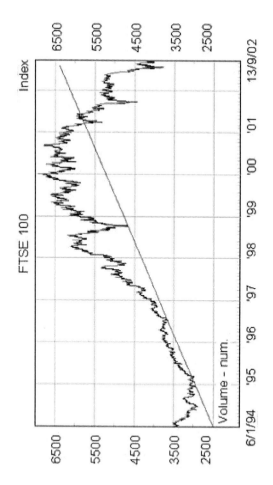

Source: *ShareScope*

5.6 Trendlines - An End To Emotional Decision

Using trendlines have the added bonus of removing emotional decisions from analytical decisions. In other words, there is no need to say, "I think it's time to sell…" (an emotional decision). Instead you can make your decision from an analytical point of view, eg, "I will hold until the current upward trend is broken."

5.7 Summary - Trends and Using Trendlines

Markets move in trends. Once a trend has been identified all you need to do is bet with the trend, up or down. There is no need to attempt to predict the trends. Your aim is simply to follow them. Even understanding the reason why a share or index is moving up or down is unnecessary. The key point is that the price is telling you what is really happening.

The longer any given trend lasts the more significant it becomes. This will be demonstrated by several 'touches' on the trendline. When a long term trendline is broken be prepared for a significant reversal in the trend.

Trendlines will almost always keep you on the right side of the market. If you keep your discipline and use trendlines properly, you will not be able to stay long when prices are falling. Similarly you will not stay short when prices are rising because in both instances the trendline will be broken.

It is also worth remembering that this strategy is not designed to pick the exact bottom or the exact top of a trend. The important element is to be trading with the trend between those points. That's where you will make profit.

5.8 Moving Averages

Having grasped the concept that markets move in trends, let's look at another money making trading strategy - the simple moving average (often referred to as SMA).

A simple moving average is calculated by adding up the closing prices of a share or index for a given number of days and dividing their total by the number of days.

For example:

A 5 day moving average would be calculated as follows:

Days	Price
1	356
2	351
3	364
4	370
5	368
Total	1809

The simple moving average for the 5 days would therefore be:

1809 divided by 5 = 361.8

The above is intended for demonstration purposes only as performing such calculations yourself is unnecessary. Computers and charting software can produce moving averages in seconds and when plotted on a chart they provide very valuable information.

As you have already seen in the previous section, the chart of any share or index will often produces erratic movement.

Take a look at the chart below of Vodafone Group PLC. This is a normal chart of the share price over a 5 year period. Running with the price you can see a line. This is a Simple Moving Average (in this case a 200 day moving average).

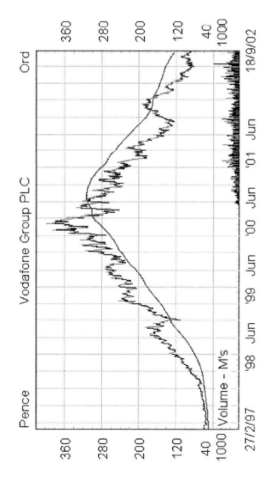

Source: *ShareScope*

AN INTRODUCTION TO FINANCIAL SPREAD BETTING

5.9 Buy and Sell Signals

The obvious question when using moving averages is when to buy and when to sell. Probably the most effective way of interpreting a moving average is to compare the relationship between a moving average of the share price with the share's price itself.

Using this trading strategy, a buy signal is indicated when the share price rises above its moving average and a sell signal is indicated when the share price falls below its moving average. As you can see in the Vodafone example above, this trading strategy proved very effective and very profitable. A buy signal was indicated as the share price moved above the 200 day moving average and performed consistently staying above the simple moving average from 1997 until 2000. In March 2000 the share price fell below the moving average indicating a sell signal and continued to fall to below 100p in 2002.

5.10 Moving Averages - Number of Days?

When deciding on the type of moving average you are going to use it is worth remembering that this will largely depend on whether you are trading a longer or shorter contract.

As a general rule of thumb the 200 day moving average is most suitable for long term trading of 100-200 days. For medium term trades from between 35 - 100 days, the 50 day moving average is probably your best indicator and for short term trades of say, between 14 and 30 days, a 20 day moving average.

5.11 Combining Moving Averages

Buy and sell signals can also be generated on a chart by combining moving averages. This trading strategy involves plotting two different moving averages on the chart. In this case I have used a 50 day and a 200 day simple day moving average. (As I have already mentioned, all charting software uses moving averages and will do this for you in just a few seconds).

When the 50 day moving average crosses and moves up through the 200 day moving average a buy signal is created (known as a 'golden cross'). When the 50 day moving average falls, crosses and moves below the 200 day moving average a sell signal is created (a 'dead cross').

In the following three examples see how the 50 day moving average (thin line) behaves in relation to the 200 day moving average (thicker line) creating buy and sell signals.

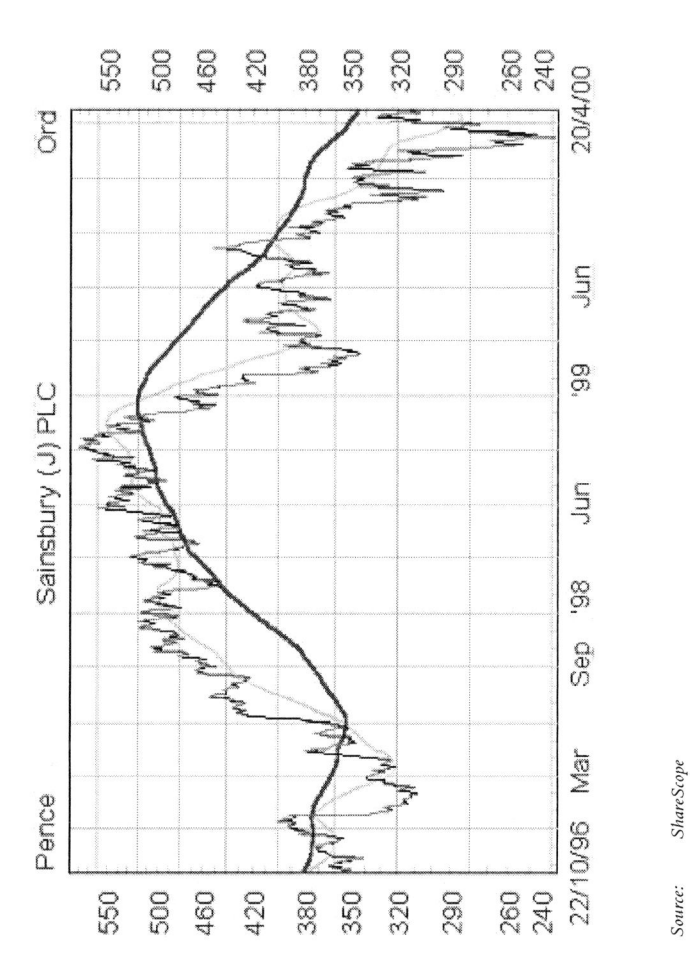

Source: ShareScope

The 50 day simple moving average crosses the 200 day moving average in June 1997 when Sainsbury shares are trading at 364p. The shares reach a peak of 580p in October 1998 before falling. In December 1998 the 50 day moving average falls through the 200 day moving producing a sell signal at 483p. By March 2000 the shares have reached a low of 239p.

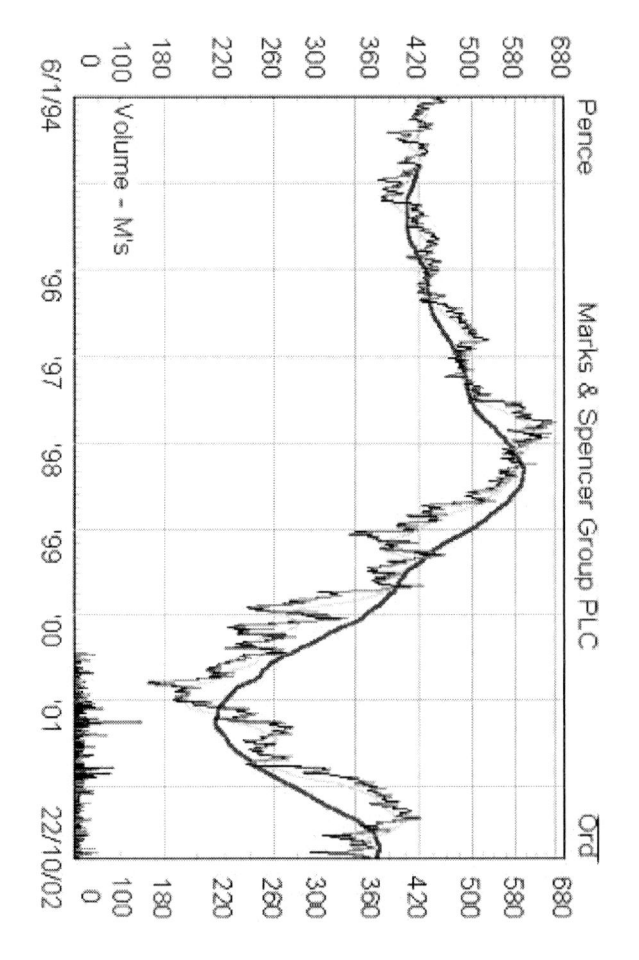

Source: ShareScope

Note how the Marks & Spencer share price moves in line with the 50 day moving average from 1995 until the end of 1997, rising from below 400p to a peak of 651p in October 1997. In April 1998 the 50 day moving average falls below the 200 day moving average creating a sell signal at around 591p. The share price continues to fall until 2001. The 50 day moving average moves up above the 200 day moving average in March 2001 at 234p.

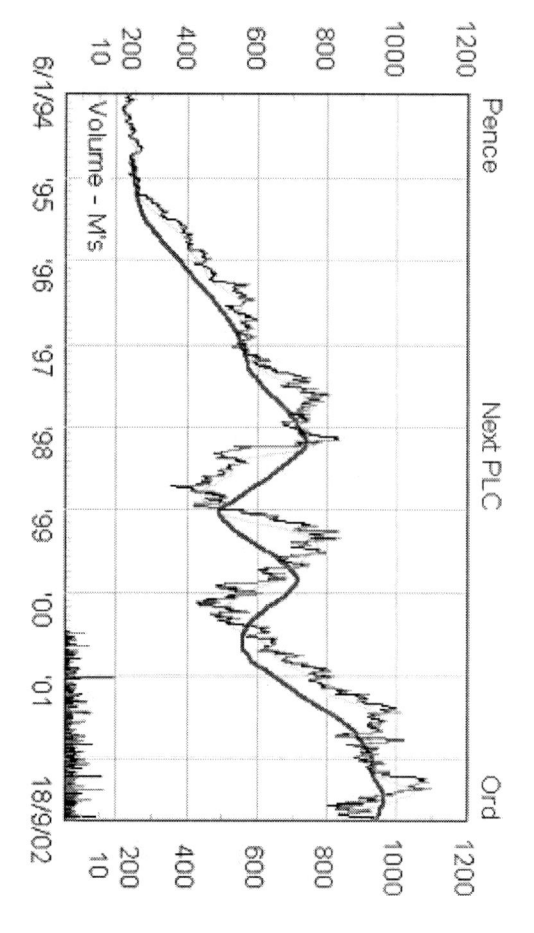

Source: *ShareScope*

The chart for the shares of Next PLC again shows rises and falls with the 50 day moving average providing buy and sell signals as it falls and rises through the 200 day moving average.

5.12 Summary - Moving Averages

Like using trends and trendlines, a moving average trading system is not designed to get you in at the exact bottom or the exact top. Instead, it is a very effective system of keeping you in line with a share price trend by buying shortly after the share price bottoms and selling shortly after the share price tops.

Another advantage of this strategy is that losses are always cut short because positions must be closed when the price breaks through the moving average. Profits, on the other hand, are allowed to run. In many instances big up or down movement in a share price or index can last for weeks, months or even years. This strategy, by its very nature, enables you to profit from the big proportion of the middle of the move. As long as the move prevails you continue to hold and watch your profit grow.

5.13 Exit Signals With A Trailing Stop

As discussed in the last section, the moving average trading system gives a clear exit signal. If you follow the rules, once the price moves through the moving average you close your position.

Another system based on a similar principle is shown below.
Here you have a chart for Debenhams PLC from November
2000 to August 2001. Below the price you will see another line.
This is a trailing stop set at 15% below the price. Note how this
trailing stop keeps you in the trade until the line is hit at the end
of July 2001 at around 400p mark. This is your exit signal.

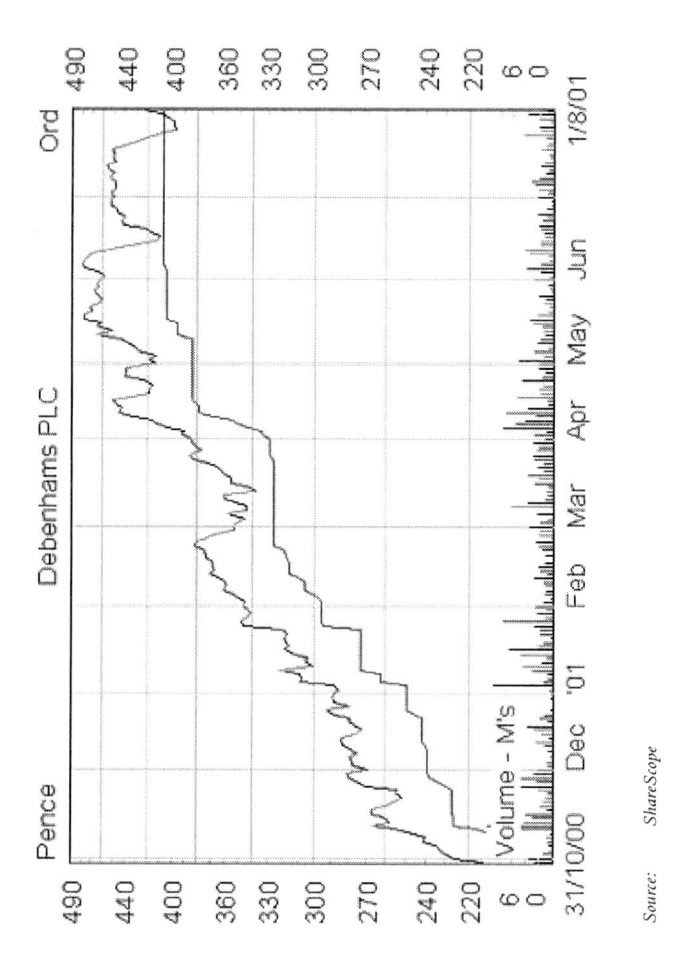

The chart below shows how the price of Debenhams PLC shares subsequently fell to below 200p by October 2002.

Like the moving average trading system, trailing a stop in this way helps take the emotion out of the trade. You have a mechanical exit rule. Follow it and the decision to exit the trade is made for you.

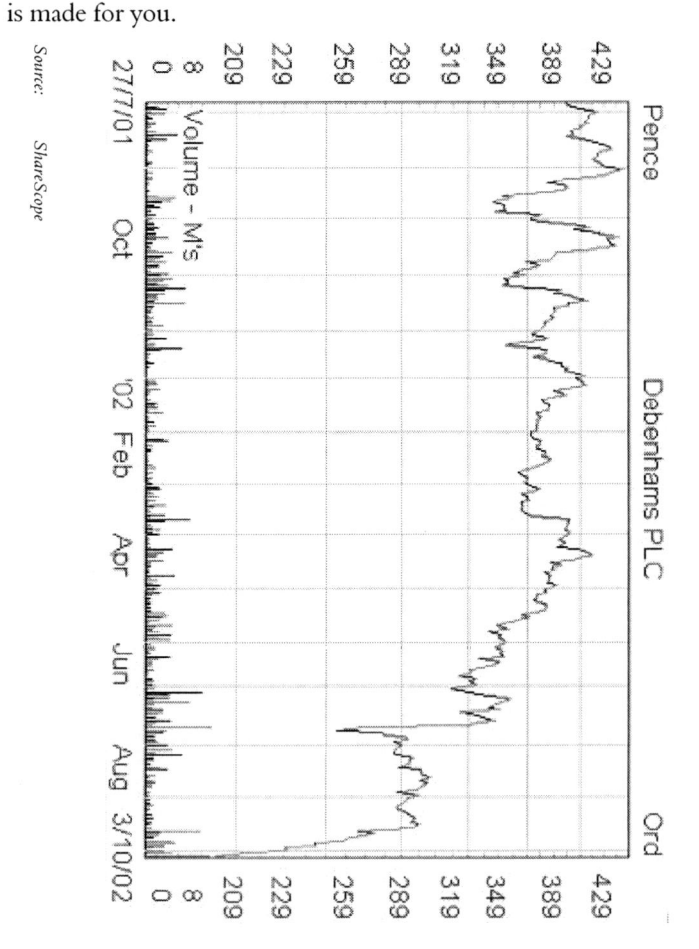

Source: ShareScope

5.14 Support and Resistance Levels

We are now going to take a look at support and resistance levels. It's another tool worth adding to your armoury in the quest to make you a winner. So far in this chapter we have discussed the use of trend trading systems, moving average trading systems and trailing stops. However when dealing with 'range' markets, these style trading systems become difficult to apply. This is when a support and resistance trading system comes into it's own.

Shown below is a chart for Tesco PLC. The share price rises and falls in a trading range between 196p and 156p.

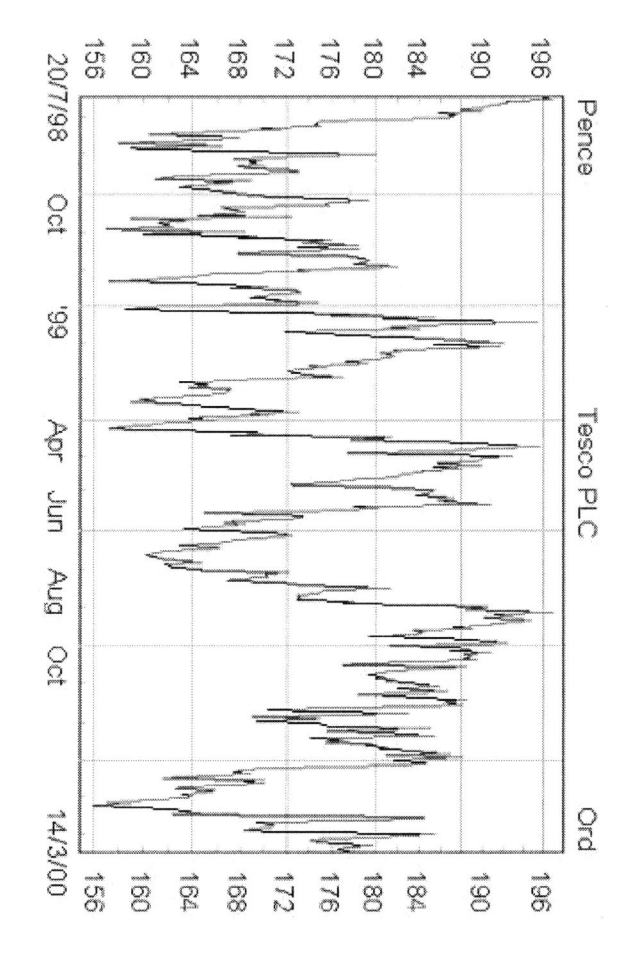

Source: *ShareScope*

The movement of the share price can be thought as a fight between buyers and sellers. The buyers push prices higher and the sellers push prices lower. The direction the price moves reveals who is winning the fight. In this example, see how during the period from July 1998 to March 2000, every time the Tesco share price fell to 156p the buyers took control and prevented the price falling lower. That meant that at the price of 156p buyers felt that investing in Tesco was worthwhile and sellers were not willing to sell for less than 156p. This type of price action is called support, because buyers are supporting the price at 156p.

Similar to support, a resistance level is the point at which sellers take control of the price and stop it from rising higher. Each time the price reaches 196p, sellers outnumber buyers and stop the price from rising.

The price at which a trade takes place is the price at which a buyer and a seller agree to do business. It represents the consensus of their expectations for the share. The buyer thinks the price will go up and the seller thinks the price will go down.

Support levels indicate the price at which the majority of investors believe that prices will go up and resistance levels indicate the price at which the majority of investors think the price will go down. The support level (lower) and resistance level (higher) have been drawn in on the chart below.

Of course, in time, investor expectations change. And when they do, the share price often moves significantly. Note how when the price breaks through the resistance level, the share price moves up sharply. The buyers have won the fight and taken control (the sellers resistance has been broken). The majority of investors now think the share price will go up and buyers push it up to 276p by November 2000.

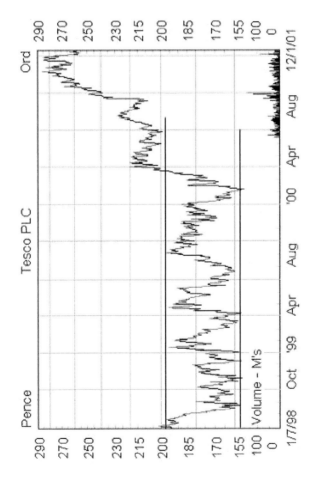

Source: ShareScope

5.15 Chart Breakouts - New Highs and New Lows

Although logic would suggest that the way to make money would be to buy low and sell high, more often than not shares that are low, go lower and shares that are high, go higher.

In the example below of ICAP PLC you will see a line drawn to indicate where the share reaches an all time high towards the end of 2000. Many, perhaps, would have thought this the time to sell when in fact the correct view was to buy. You would have been buying at an all time high but as you can see the share continued to reach new highs.

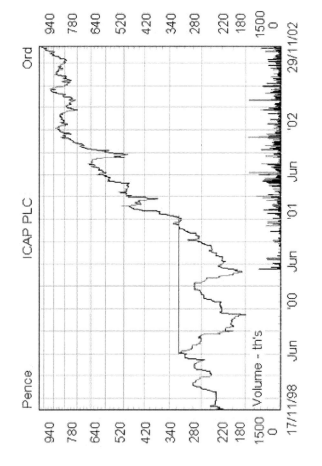

Source: ShareScope

5.16 52 Week - Highs and Lows

Most computer software packages (see below) have a filter that allows you to view a list of all the new highs and lows. The Financial Times also provides a list of companies that have made new highs in which sector.

No.	Name	Close	Consensus	Close +/-	Price %	Price high	Price low	Capita (£m)	EPS	Divi	P/E	PEG
2	Eckoh Technologies	12¼p		1½p	13.95	12¼p	5p	25.3	-5.6			
3	Huntingdon Life Sciences	4½p		½p	12.5	4½p	2¾p					
4	ComputerLand UK	81½p		8p	10.88	81½p	45p	8.2	5.2	2.2	15.7	
5	Character Group	51½p	Buy	5p	10.75	51½p	18½p	21.3	-23.5			
6	Torday & Carlisle	40p		3½p	9.59	40p	20p	9	4.4	0.5	9.2	
7	Orbital Software	27p		1½p	5.88	27p	25½p					
8	Air Music & Media	6½p		¼p	4	6½p	4½p	9.1	19.9		0.3	
9	Carr's Milling	£2.48½	Buy	9½p	3.97	£2.48½	£1.29	20	17.3	9.5	14.4	
10	NHP PLC	98p	Buy	3p	3.16	98p	45½p	196.8	11.4		8.6	
11	GW Pharmaceuticals	£1.52½	Buy	4½p	3.04	£1.52½	81p	152.7	-8.9			
12	Excel Airways	£1.43		3p	2.14	£1.43	£1.20	137.3	122		1.2	0
13	Atrium Underwriting PLC	99½p	Strong hold	2p	2.05	99½p	66p	48.4	-32.6			
14	Radstone Technology	£2.79½	Buy	4p	1.45	£2.79½	£1.91½	66.6	13.9	1	20.1	0.93
15	Sherry FitzGerald	79½p	Buy	1p	1.27	79½p	57p	10.6	3.5	1	36.4	0.06
16	Hardy Underwriting	£2.01½	Buy	1½p	0.75	£2.01½	£1.41½	70.9	15.8	6.2	12.8	4.21
17	Ennstone PLC	36¾p		¼p	0.68	36¾p	29¼p	59.9	3	0.9	12.2	4.08
18	Parthusceva	£4.35		2½p	0.58	£4.35	£2.75					

Source: *ShareScope*

AN INTRODUCTION TO FINANCIAL SPREAD BETTING

Chapter 6

SOME MORE TIPS…AND A LITTLE PSYCHOLOGY

6.1 Watch Directors' Dealing

The directors of a business are, or should be, in the best position to know what the real state of a business is. Watch how the directors, and other key employees, buy and sell shares. Beware when directors say they are selling shares to create 'liquidity' in the stock. It may just be a 'smokescreen' and an attempt to hide the true state of the business. On the other hand, when directors buy shares, it can be a good signal that the business is in much better shape than the market is predicting.

For small and medium sized companies, be slightly sceptical if the directors don't own a stake in the business. If they are not shareholders themselves, their motivation to grow the share price could justifiably be questioned.

The Financial Times has a regular column detailing directors dealing and most Sunday newspapers feature one company's share transactions by directors, graphing the share price accordingly.

6.2 The Grey Suit Story

In some ways the stock market is really no different from owning a business. Trading is a business and should be operated like one.

For example, take a men's clothing shop. The owner stocks the men's suits in three colours - grey, blue and brown. The grey suits are quickly sold out, the blue suits are half sold and the brown suits have not sold at all. What should he do?

Does he go to his buyer and say, "The grey suits are all sold out. The brown suits don't seem to have any demand but I still think they are good and anyway, brown is my favourite colour, so let's buy some more brown suits anyway"?

No, of course not.

> The clever shopkeeper who survives in the retail business eyes this predicament objectively and says, "I've made a mistake. I'd better get rid of the brown suits. I'll mark them down 15%. Let's have a sale. And if they don't go at that price I'll mark them down to 20%, then 25%. I'll get my money out of the brown suits and invest it into the fast moving grey suits that are in demand."
>
> This is common sense in a retail business. The same principle can be applied to trading.

6.3 Profit Warnings

When a company announces a profits warning, there is a very good chance it won't be the last. In fact, profit warnings rarely seem to arrive in anything less that threes. A possible explanation for this is that whilst it takes years to build up the momentum of a really successful company, once a setback occurs, directors are forced onto the back foot and often find it extremely difficult to regain momentum.

6.4 Watch Wall Street

The UK stock market is often affected by rises and falls in the US, so it is advisable to keep an eye on Wall Street. For example, if the Dow Jones Industrial Average falls on any given day (Wall Street closes at 9.00pm UK time) the chances are that the FTSE 100 will open lower the following day.

Take a look at the two charts below over a five year period showing how the FTSE 100 closely follows the Dow Jones.

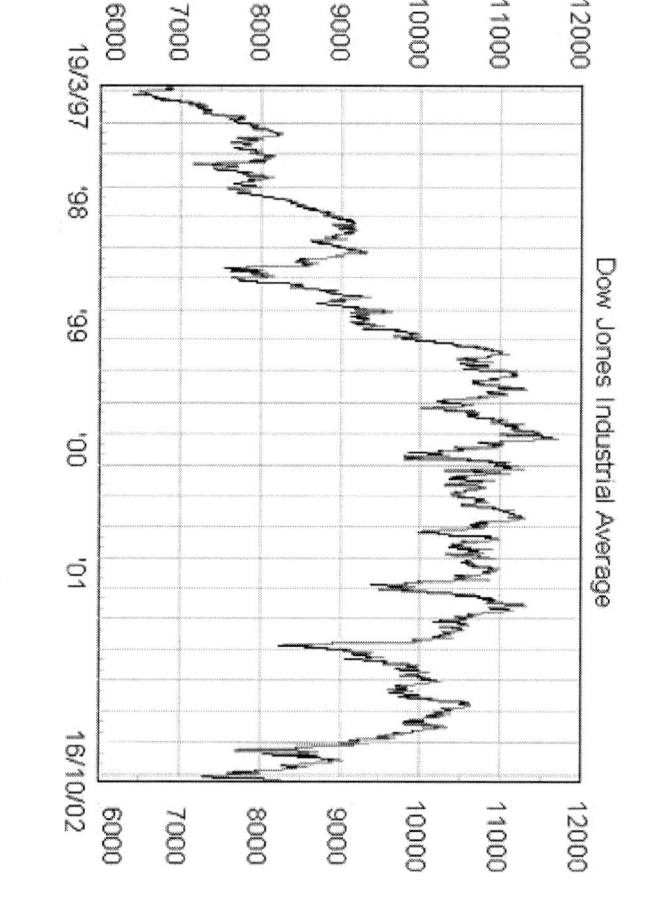

Source:

ShareScope

SOME MORE TIPS...AND A LITTLE PSYCHOLOGY

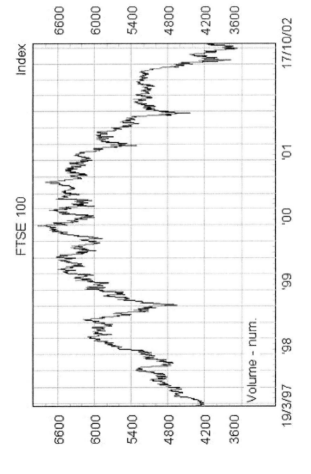

Source: *ShareScope*

6.5 Cut Trades That Go Wrong

If you are expecting a bet to move your way and it goes wrong then you should close your position. Remember, your first loss is almost always the smallest. Similarly, if you have placed a stop and your bet goes wrong and the price starts to move towards it you should never move your stop unless you have a very good reason.

6.6 Cutting Losses Is like Buying an Insurance Policy

The policy of limiting losses is similar to paying an insurance premium. You reduce your risk to exactly the amount you are willing to take. Of course, sometimes you will see the share you have cut short turn around and go up. You will probably get very annoyed and think you made a bad decision but this is the wrong way to look at the situation.

Take another view. If you bought insurance on your car last year and didn't have an accident, did you waste your money? Are you going to buy the car insurance this year. Of course you are!

Did you buy fire insurance on your home last year. If your home did not burn down last year, are you upset because you made a bad financial decision?

> You don't buy fire insurance because you know your house is going to burn down. You buy insurance just in case, to protect you from the remote possibility of a serious loss. It is the same for the winning trader who cuts losses quickly and closely. He or she wants to protect against the possible chance of a larger potentially devastating loss from which it may not be possible to recover.
>
> Small loses are cheap insurance and the only kind of insurance you can buy on your investment. Even if a number of the shares move up after you sell, which many of them surely will, you have accomplished your critical objective of keeping all your losses small. And you still have your money to try again for a winner in another share.

6.7 Trade Active Shares

There are thousands of companies listed on the stock market both in the UK and the US. However, many of these shares do not move a great deal. This is usually a sign that the volume of shares traded is low. You should be looking to trade a active shares, those with significant daily volume. Also you will find that the most active shares such as Vodafone and BP have the tightest spreads.

6.8 Add To Winning Bets

Place small bets (the minimum bet size) and add to your position if the bet proves to be a winner. Building up your position this way also helps you to run your winning bets. For many holding a winning bet is as distressing as holding a losing bet. However, this is something you must do. To be successful it is vital to run winners more than you run losers. Never add to losing bets.

6.9 Trade With A Plan

You must have a plan. Many losing traders do not. They do not define the risks, have no profit objectives and simply dive in head first! If they do have a plan, they don't stick to it. This is particularly true when the bet is a loser. They base their decisions on hunches and long shots rather than sound fundamental and technical reasoning. They often bet too much money and fail to use stops.

6.10 Overconfidence

Usually after a series of successes there is a danger of becoming overconfident. Because previous bets have been so profitable and exciting you view your next trade as another 'big killing' and bet too much money. This invariably results in a losing bet.

Afterwards you will almost certainly be able to look back and identify your mistake - that your bet was based on overconfidence and little else.

Your aim should be to profit regularly with consistent bets at a level of money you feel comfortable with and not to make a killing in one big hit. If you can avoid this temptation, you will save yourself a great deal of money and considerably improve your chances of success.

6.11 Newspaper Stories

In most cases, news that appears in the press has already been taken into account by the stock market. Many new traders jump into a market purely on the basis of a story they have read in a newspaper not realising that the market has already discounted the information.

6.12 Overtrading

Newcomers often overtrade. They open a betting account and become like a child with a new toy. They want to trade anything and everything. They frequently open too many positions.

6.13 Failure To Take A Loss

Many traders refuse to cut their losses. Rather than take a small loss, they stick with a losing trade until it develops into a heavy loss - and then take the loss. This is a very undisciplined approach and must be avoided. You need to develop a system and stick to the rules rigidly.

6.14 Always Betting Up

Many traders have a directional bias - usually up. They are always looking to be long and will not consider going short. A successful trader is happy to bet up or down.

6.15 Greed

Some traders will allow winning bets to dwindle into losing bets while hoping for larger profits.

6.15 The Chicken Story

An Analogy of the Psychology of the 'Average Trader'
It's a beautiful sunny afternoon and a young boy goes off for a walk in the countryside. He approaches a farm and at the gates comes across an old man trying to catch chickens. He has a chicken trap, a makeshift device which consists of a large box with the door hinged at the top. This door is kept open by a stick to which is tied a piece of string leading back around twenty metres to the old man hiding behind a tree. A thin trail of corn is scattered along a path leading the chickens to the box. Once inside the chickens have an even more plentiful supply of corn.

When enough chickens have wandered inside the box, the old man would pull the stick away and let the door fall shut. Once shut, the door couldn't be open again without going up to the box and this would scare away any chickens lurking outside. The time to pull away the stick is when as many chickens are inside as one can reasonably expect. Soon the old man has ten chickens inside the box. Then one wanders out, leaving nine.

"Damn, I wish I had pulled the string when all ten were in the box," says the old man, "perhaps I'll wait a minute to see if the other one goes back in."

But while he waits for the tenth chicken to return, two more walk out.

"I should have been satisfied with nine," curses the old man, "just as soon as I get one more back I'll pull the string."

But three more walk out. Still the man waits. Having once had ten, he dislikes going home with less than six. He simply can't give up the idea that some of the original number will return. When finally only one chicken remains in the trap he says, "I'll wait until he walks out or another goes in, and then I'll quit."

The solitary chicken goes to join the others and the old man returns home empty handed.

Epilogue

THE GOLDEN RULES OF FINANCIAL SPREAD BETTING

Rule 1 - Begin Paper Trading

Before rushing off to the telephone to call your bookmaker, plan some make believe bets. Try to make your paper trading as realistic as possible. Watch the market and make your decision as carefully as possible, imaging that you are using real money and write the bet down.

For example, you buy £20 March FTSE at 4200. Now watch the market and decide when to close your bet or to let the bet run.

Rule 2 - Take Control

The ability to control your emotions and to maintain an objective temperament are vital ingredients if you are going to be a winner. Losing your cool is a recipe for disaster. Those who have a personality that will allow them to remain unemotional about their positions are far more likely to succeed. With the market subject to numerous fluctuations on a daily basis it takes a great deal of discipline and an ability to look beyond short term events to avoid the temptation of changing your mind and your position every few minutes.

Rule 3 - Start Small

When you have gained some confidence from trading on paper, begin by betting the minimum bet size. This for most bookmakers is £2 a point. It does not matter if you only make a small amount, the important factor is that you will be gaining experience and learning to read the market correctly.

Rule 4 - Only Use Money You Can Afford To Lose

As harsh as this may sound, you really should only be betting money you can afford to lose. If you are betting with money that you need for other things you are certain to fail. You simply will not be able to make sound decisions if you are betting with money you are terrified of losing.

Rule 5 - Cut Your Loses Short

Nobody likes to admit they are wrong! This fact makes cutting your loses one of the most difficult things to do - it takes a huge amount of discipline. But unless you learn this golden rule you are not going to survive in the world of financial spread betting. New traders, in particular, often find admitting that they are wrong an almost impossible task and simply refuse to close losing bets leading to even greater loses.

Cutting your loses short is an essential part of your money management. Even if you are correct on less than half of your trades, as long as you cut your loses short and let your profits run, you can still make money. Having three or four winning bets out of ten can make you a winner if you keep your discipline.

Rule 6 - Let Your Profits Run

It is important to let a profitable position run and not to close your bet too early. Sometimes it may be tempting to close a position just for the sake of taking a profit. Resist this urge. Ask yourself why you want to close the bet? You may be throwing away even more profit by closing your bet too soon. (Review Chapter 5 and see how the moving average trading strategy and trailing a stop keep you in the winning trades).

Rule 7 - Don't Get In The Way Of Trends (Trains)

When a market is moving in a major trend, think of it as a speeding train - and don't get in the way. If you do, you are likely to get hurt. A mistake often made by those new to financial spread betting is to buy or be long in a down trend or sell short in an up trend.

Rule 8 - Take A Break

Most new traders have the urge to trade every day. The more sensible approach is to take a break every now and then, particularly when going through a losing patch. Close your trades and look at the position again.

Rule 9 - Don't Trade Everything At Once

To begin with it is advisable to trade one market only. Then as your confidence builds you may wish to look at other markets, trading with the minimum bet size.

Rule 10 - Beware Of Too Much Information

The danger of having too much information is that you can easily be influenced by what others say. On the various financial TV news channels, in the newspapers and magazines you will be subject to numerous market commentators giving their opinions on the markets.

Don't always be influenced by what others say or you will be changing your mind all the time. Once you have formed your own opinion on market direction, it is often more profitable to 'stick to your guns' and hold your position.

Rule 11 - Act Promptly

Markets can be cruel to those who procrastinate. This does not mean you should act impulsively but it is usually a good idea to act promptly. If your judgement is telling you to liquidate a position - do so - don't wait another minute. Similarly, when ready to trade - act now.

Rule 12 - Learn To Sell Short

Most people do not understand that you can make money by betting a market will go down. In many cases, markets actually fall faster than they rise and you can often earn quick profits by selling short.

Rule 13 - Always Take Windfall Profits

On occasions, within a few hours of placing a trade, you will find yourself with more profit than you ever expected. Do not be tempted to wait a few more days to work out why the profit came so fast. Just take the quick profit and don't ask questions.

Rule 14 - Stick With The Trend

Major price trends can be identified with technical analysis (chapter 5). The mistake many traders make is to go against the trend. They buy when the market is in a basic down trend, or sell when there is an up trend.

Glossary

BALANCE OF PAYMENTS
Measurement of imports and exports in and out of the country.

BULL
One who expects process to rise. A bullish view.

BULL MARKET
A market in which prices are rising.

BEAR
One who expects the market to fall. A bearish view.

BEAR MARKET
A market in which prices are falling.

CAC 40
Index of Euronext Paris, French Stock Exchange.

CHARTIST
Someone who studies technical analysis.

CONTRACT MONTH

The month in which spread bets must be settled.

CONTROLLED RISK BET

A bet which has a strictly limited maximum loss.

DAX

Index of Deutsche Borse, German Stock Exchange.

DIRECTORS

The managers of a company appointed by the shareholders.

DIVIDEND YIELD

The yield on a share defined as:

$$\frac{\text{Dividend per share}}{\text{Current market price per share}} = X\ 100\%$$

DOW JONES INDEX

Index of the New York Stock Exchange.

DOWNTREND

A price trend characterised by a series of lower highs and lower lows.

EARNINGS PER SHARE

$$\frac{\text{Profits after tax}}{\text{Number of Ordinary Shares in Issue}}$$

EXPIRATION DATE
The last day that a spread bet may be traded.

EXPIRE
Letting a spread bet expire without closing the trade.

FTSE 100 INDEX
Index of the largest 100 listed companies on the London Stock Exchange.

FUNDAMENTAL ANALYSIS
The analysis of a company and the industry in which it operates to make buy or sell decisions.

GOOD TIL CANCELLED
An order that remains in effect until it is cancelled.

HANG SENG INDEX
Index of the Hong Kong Stock Exchange.

LIQUIDITY
The ease with which a share can be converted into cash. Some smaller company' shares are said to be illiquid whereas a share such as Barclays or Vodaphone is very liquid.

LONG
One who has placed a spread bet with a view that the price will rise.

NIKKEI 225 INDEX
Index of the Tokyo Stock Exchange.

PRICE EARNING RATIO

Market price per share
‾‾‾‾‾‾‾‾‾‾‾‾‾‾‾‾‾‾‾‾
  Earnings per share

SHORT
One who has placed a spread bet with a view that the price will fall.

SPREAD
The difference between the buying and selling price for a particular bet. This is how the bookmaker makes a profit.

STANDARD AND POORS 500 (S & P)
Index of the New York Stock Exchange.

STOPPED OUT
When the bookmaker's quote hits the specific stop loss level you set.

TECHNICAL ANALYSIS
The analysis of share prices and making buy or sell decisions on the basis of trends in price movements.

UPTREND
A price trend characterised by a series of higher highs and higher lows.

Appendix

THE PSYCHOLOGY OF TRADING

Ask yourself why you purchased this publication in the first place, and why now you are reading this article. Possibly it is for purely intellectual interest, but more likely it is because you are interested in trading financial markets. Why? To take control of our own financial future after three years of excuses from fund managers, whilst all our retirements get closer. So we are looking to make money and have some fun and excitement in the process.

For over 17 years I have been actively involved in trading, as a professional dealer for large US and Japanese investment banks, whilst also trading for my own account, and now as Managing Director of Cantor Index, the fastest growing spread betting company in the market. Throughout these years I have had the opportunity to observe and learn from my professional colleagues, my own private and professional trading and far more importantly, I have been able to study the trading styles and patterns of many thousands of clients now spread betting with Cantor Index. Whether the trader is a professional at a bank or a private spread better, there are recurring themes and traits that would appear to clearly differentiate the winners from the losers. By understanding and applying these traits to your own trading might improve your chances of beating the markets over time.

Interest in trading has continued to grow since the concept of day trading arrived from the US and intensified during the tech stock boom at the end of the nineties. Those heady days are way behind us now, and although stock markets have been in decline for the last 3 years the popularity and necessity of trading (rather than investing) continues to grow.

As mentioned above, I believe this is in part due to the fact that people now want control of their own money as numerous scandals have rocked financial institutions with miss-selling of pensions and endowments, the split-cap funds debacle and the general poor performance of managed investments, all of which has led to many people losing faith in the institutions they once trusted with their hard earned cash.

If any of us were asked why we are interested in trading our first response would probably be that it gives us the opportunity to make money. That is a good enough reason in itself but that is not the complete answer. There is another vital factor that adds to our desire to trade. We love the buzz. Trading gives us a huge adrenaline rush. Betting on a horse race, a playing card, or a roulette number can be exciting, but its over in a few minutes.

Financial markets are "running" all day, 5 days a week, constantly changing. So we want to make money and we enjoy the excitement, both very human emotions. It is the addictive nature of these two drivers that makes trading financial markets at the same time compelling and so very difficult.

So we have established why we might want to trade financial markets, but how would we describe these markets? Students of economics will tell us that markets are "where large numbers of buyers and sellers, all of them small, so that they act as price takers, with complete information and rational expectations transact their business." That may be the theoretical definition, but does that match up to reality. In my experience very few participants have complete information and even less have rational expectations. A cold theoretical statement cannot possibly sum up the frantic, wild, frustrating, satisfying, scary place that the markets can be. Think along the lines of a Saloon bar in the Wild West or a boxing ring and you might be closer to the hostile world of financial markets. They are dangerous, unpredictable and unforgiving, and never more so than the time when you delude yourself that you can understand, predict, or tame them.

You get the picture. The markets can and will surprise everyone at some stage. You can be right or wrong and not know the reason why. Don't think a stock can't double in price, it can and don't think it can't half in price, it can and will when you least expect it. The market will move in a way to cause the most pain to the most people. You are entering an environment you cannot hope to control, but you can and must control your own behaviour, and there lies, perhaps, the secret to having a chance of coming out on top.

With all this talk of such a volatile and unpredictable market you could be forgiven for thinking that there is little value in attempting to make reasoned decisions. In general some analysis is preferable to relying simply upon hope and prayer. Whatever techniques and sources you draw upon to make your decisions, be they from the press, television, the internet, charts, research, advice, rumour, gut feeling, etc., it is essential to realise that how ever solid that view may feel, the markets can prove you wrong in a heartbeat. So have some kind of plan before opening a position base upon possible scenarios. It is, however, the case that plans are not enough; first we must understand ourselves, and how we are likely to react to unforeseen market behaviour.

It is a fact of human nature that we are generally risk averse individuals who therefore never want to risk too much, and that we are dominated by irrational behaviour driven by the hope of winning (how ever unlikely) a larger prize, than another more efficient option with smaller prizes. This can be witnessed at your local newsagent every week. A low risk outlay of £1 for a lottery ticket is taken in the irrational hope, ie, 14,000,000/1 of winning the large prize of around £6 million. A very poor value trade indeed. But neither would we take the other side of this bet, in fear in losing millions of pounds.

But, not only are we risk averse and irrational, we have that added handicap of being emotional; driven by fear and greed. The fear of losing results in our aversion to risk, and our irrational behaviour is driven by our greed. Bearing all this in mind, what do we need to be a successful market operator? There are numerous qualities we can list that might help us to be successful traders, such as; ignore our emotions; maintain a developed trading style; maintain and understand risk; good timing; remain focused and objective; never over trade; remain comfortable shorting the markets and, of course never forgetting a little luck. But in truth it really boils down to just two basic traits that encapsulate those listed above, which are necessary to help us beat the market; avoiding greed and fear, and maintaining strong self discipline. Given that the secret to avoiding the emotions of greed and fear is self control, why don't we simply identify "discipline" as the single attribute to being a successful trader in financial markets.

To avoid greed and fear, to take the emotion out of our trading, we need to remain calm, which is clearly far easier said than done. If you have ever visited a futures trading pit you will know the first thing to hit you is the tremendous noise. Just think, this market where the world's largest financial institutions use their vast analytical resources to trade billions of dollars worth of financial instruments all comes down to a group of large men (and a few women) bellowing and gesticulating at each other. The sound is exhilarating; one cannot help but be caught up in the wild, bordering on panic, atmosphere.

Through the late eighties and early nineties I worked in the dealing room of a large American investment bank, full of squawk boxes from the futures pit; the noise would fill the dealing room, spreading the frantic atmosphere, creating an unlikely environment for sound rational decisions. Later I moved to a Japanese bank where squawk boxes in the dealing room were banned; the difference in atmosphere was remarkable. The markets were, of course, still just as volatile, but the calm environment was far more conducive to making my own decisions in a more composed fashion, without the accompaniment of screaming pit traders. Although you will not have to worry about the hubbub of squawk boxes influencing your trading, the principal of keeping calm in the good times and the bad times remains.

When we decide to buy or sell, our judgement is on the line. When a stock we have bought is going up it confirms how good our judgement is. We know how to pick these stocks, no problem. The stock price continues to rise, we fear if we sell now we will miss out on further profits. Our greed tells us to hang on for an ever higher price. We might just as easily have sold too early in the fear that the small unrealised profit might quickly reverse into a loss.

But if the market is running against us, what does that say about our judgement? There is a feeling of wounded pride. A lot of time was spent researching that stock, "I must be right; I've uncovered a gem of a stock, anyone who is selling it must be mad". The reluctance of taking a loss prevents us from closing the trade. The greed makes us hang on in the hope the price will return to the break-even level at least. But as the price continues to fall, the fear that this can only get worse and worse pushes us to get out before the price completely collapses, probably at or close to a short term bottom. If you trade like this you will quickly become burnt out, emotionally and financially.

We must always look at our positions objectively, and remember the different factors that led you to decide that a stock meets enough of your criteria to merit entering a position and stepping into the ring. Please do not let all the careful consideration you put into deciding which stock to deal in, and why, get lost in the heat of battle. You must keep applying the same analysis to the position that you used when you first decided to enter the trade. If the stock no longer meets your criteria then its time to get out, whether the trade is in profit or in loss. However, if all the criteria for entering the trade are still in place (assuming you are being honest with yourself), then you can feel far more confident about your position when faced with adverse short-term price movements. It is therefore of utmost importance that you continuously challenge your criteria to remain sure that the trade still satisfies all your criteria. If you buy a stock on the rumour that there will be a take-over bid next week and a month later nothing has happened, should you still have that position? If you sold short a stock because the chart suggest the price had reached a resistance level, but it keeps on moving up, shouldn't you review your strategy for this stock? Plan your trade and then be sure to trade your plan.

Although we need to overcome our own fear and greed, it can be very useful (perhaps necessary) to be aware of these emotions in others. The push and pull of fear and greed intensifies (and causes of course) with increased volatility, and therefore, almost by definition, will be at its worst as a market nears the top or bottom of its cycle. That is why, almost without exception, major markets will experience record volumes at the time the market reaches its low or high. It is interesting that with a market at its lowest level for many months or even years, that more sellers are available than the surrounding periods where all sell prices would have been higher. Equally the same can be seen that more buyers appear at the high of the markets than at price levels on all other days that would have been more attractive for the buyer. Of course for these transactions to occur there had to be equal numbers of opposing trades, but you work out which participants were gripped in panic and which were controlled enough to sell at the highs and buy at the lows.

For example, if we look at this price chart and volume chart for the FTSE 100, it can be clearly seen that the volume is at its greatest when the price is at its lowest point. The fear and panic has spread so thoroughly that everyone who can sell has now entered the market, until there are no sellers left. From there the price can only rise, as the buyers have to pay up to find sellers and fill their orders.

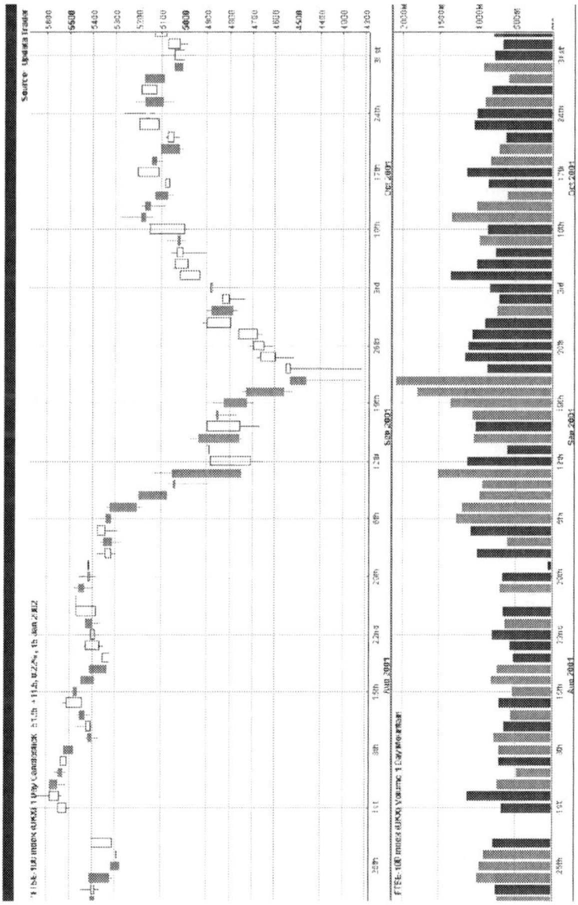
Source: Updata Trader
Aug 2001
Sep 2001
Oct 2001

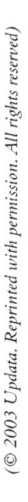

This phenomenon is also in evidence at the top of a market.

A bull (rising) market can be said to have 3 stages.

1) Disbelief - the market begins to move up, but people think the rally will be short lived. No one believes that the bear (falling) market is over so they sell into the rally.

2) Realisation - it begins to dawn on more and more participants that the market has entered a bull phase. Many traders are still reluctant to go long (buy) given that the market has moved up so far, but the short (sell) positions from lower levels can take no more pain, so begin to flatten out their positions by entering the market as a buyer. The rally continues.

3) Total belief - everyone is now certain we are in a bull market and wants to buy. Greed takes over, the buying frenzy as it begins to dawn on more and more participants that the market has entered a bull phase. As the market trades new highs more and more sellers are attracted, there are few if any shorts in the market, and the buying that powered the bull market has been diminishing for some weeks now preferring to take profits. As the sellers gain confidence there are few buyers left, and the total belief has dissipated into panic and confusion.

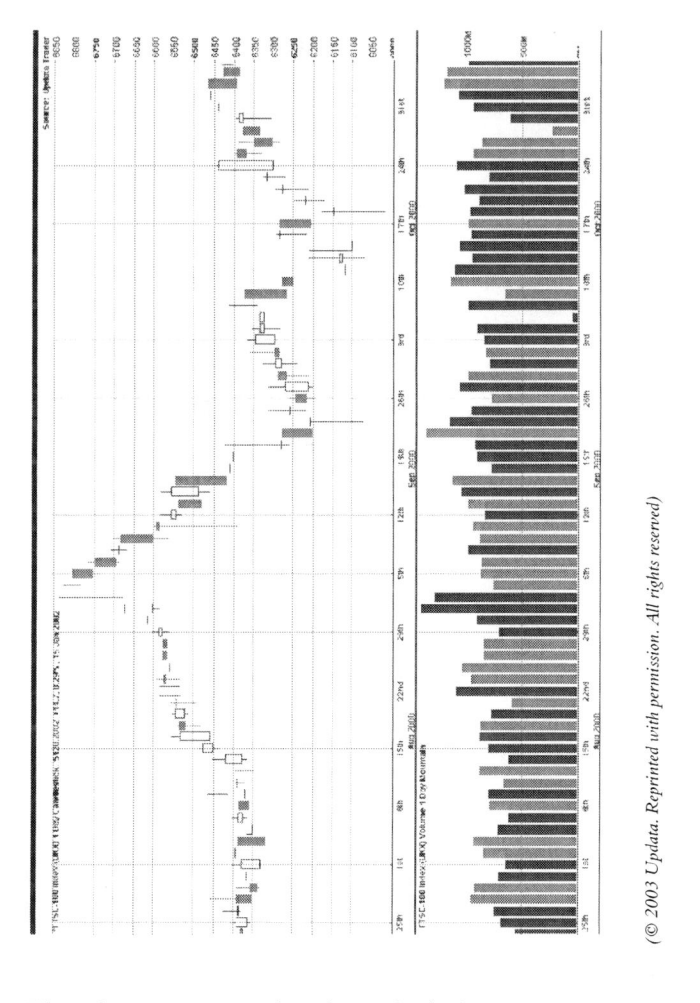

Therefore we can say that the outlook always appears worst at the lows and always great at the highs. This knowledge can help us stay detached from the hype around booming or collapsing markets. In the words of the great Warren Buffet "be fearful when others are greedy and greedy when others are fearful".

As I stated earlier, we are by nature risk adverse, our fear of risk stops us making rational decisions. Therefore if we can understand and manage risk we can start control our fear. Several factors contribute to the risks inherent in a trade:

- *Size of position* - you must understand the total exposure to the market that your position carries.
- *Tick value* - each time your chosen asset moves one point, how does that impact on your profit and loss?
- *Volatility* - have you dealt in an asset that fluctuates so violently and quickly that you dare not take your eyes away from the screen for one moment.
- *Potential losses* - What is the worst-case scenario; should your plan be totally off beam how much can you lose?
- *Probabilities of different outcomes* - Try to imagine various outcomes and plan your course of action for each one.

Having understood the risks, we also need to think about how to manage them. Always be comfortable with the size of your position. You cannot hope to make rational decisions if you are a bag of nerves every time the market moves against you a couple of ticks. Which leads on to being sure to only risk money that you can afford to lose, for your own piece of mind do not risk your house, your wife's jewellery and the kids' piggy bank savings. In order to manage risk therefore, it is useful to have a cut off point for your open trades, a point at which you have to hold you hands up in the air and admit that your judgement this time was indeed wrong. It can be very tempting to run losing positions in the vain hope that they will come good.

Another useful tool in managing risk is the use of stop orders for losses and profits. By using stop orders we can know our maximum downside or be sure to take profits on the upside. The advantage of stops (often known as stop loss orders) to cap our potential losses is that it imposes discipline for us. We know our worst-case scenario and we are prevented from running a large loss making position. The use of stop orders to take a profit (often known as a limit order) may seem unnecessary, but they also serve a useful purpose.

For example, if you buy a stock in an engineering company in the belief that they are going to secure a large contract, how much do think that will put on the price, 5%, maybe even 10%? The problem comes if the stock does indeed rise by 10%. Greed will not let you take your profit; you think there is still more juice to be squeezed out, so you hang on. Then the price falls back and you are relieved to scramble out for any profit. A limit order placed around 7% above your opening price will mean you catch any unexpected spike in the price, you may miss the very top, but you will be sure to get a good slice of it.

One of the most over used sayings connected with trading is "buy low sell high", but I would argue that this is nonsense, and is one of the major factors that differentiates our losing clients form winning clients. I often see our clients sell for no other reason than that the market has gone up, or buy for no better reason than the fact that the market has moved down. If you had consistently bought the daily, weekly, or monthly stock market lows in the last 3 years you would have lost a fortune. Timing is essential. A more helpful reinterpretation would of course be "sell higher than you buy, buy lower than you sell". Each year I buy rubbish in the January sales for no better reason than the price appears low, and regret that decision every time.

You cannot afford to ignore trends in the market, as they are like trains; you don't have to get on every one that comes along, but for goodness sake don't try and stand in the way of it! To quote Warren Buffet once more "as a group, lemmings have a rotten image, but no individual lemming ever had a bad press". In an upward trend you would always be buying at higher levels, and glad to be doing so.

Another well-worn adage is "sell the rumour and buy the fact", which states that it may well be worth while reacting to gossip and rumour as the price action might be profitable, but do not expect the confirmation of that news to lead to further profitable price action. The chart of Zurich Insurance below demonstrates this perfectly.

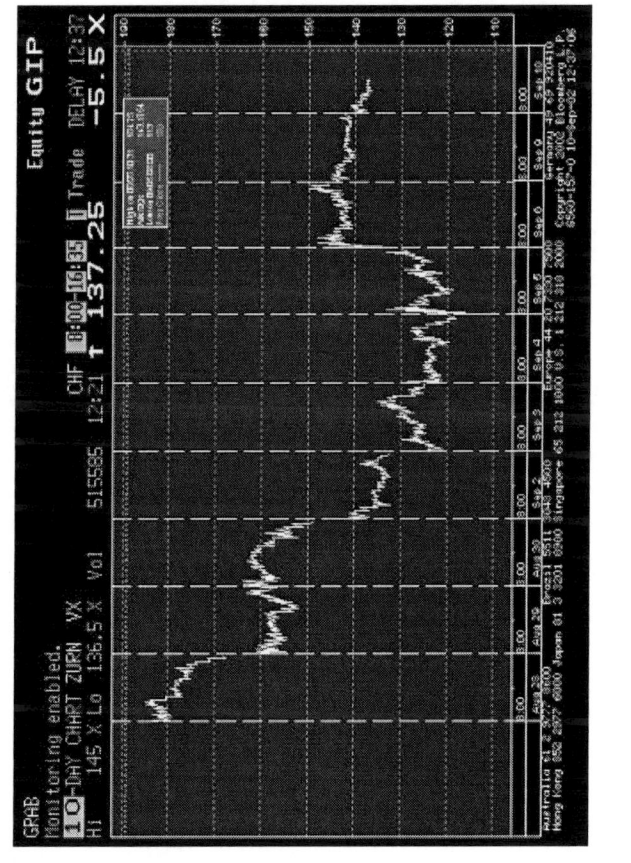

The share price tumbles amid rumours of a rights issue and poor results. The fear that disastrous news is imminent sparks a selling frenzy; everyone who can sell enters the market. Then, when the figures are announced, the fear is over. Imaginations that were running wild with thoughts of dreadful news are confronted with the facts. The market digests the news, the realisation that there are no more sellers, brings back the buyers, the shorts are squeezed and have to buy. The announcement was Thursday the 5th of September and you can see the price action either side of the news.

It is vital that you develop a trading style and rules that suit you and that you stick to them. The trading style of your friends may not be the one for you. You need to learn about yourself. It is essential to understand your appetite and attitude to risk; this takes us back to being comfortable with the size of your trades. You must know when and why you want to enter a trade and when and why you want to exit it. Remember, plan your trade and trade your plan. Do not fall into the common trap of taking a profit and running a loss. It is important to have symmetry between profits and losses. As our friend Warren Buffet once said "the advice that you never go broke taking a profit is foolish".

We must remain focused and objective at all times, once we enter the ring there is no hiding place. Always re-examine your decisions, keep re-applying your criteria to your open positions. Do not rely on hope, if it that is all you are left with, its probably too late. Why not try going flat once in a while, just for the hell of it? A long or short position often colours our view of the market in an attempt to justify our decisions. Being flat can give the chance to view the market objectively.

It is very easy to fall into the trap of over trading, something we see from our poorer performing clients. The constant desire to be involved with the markets can lead us to forget all the good habits we may have learnt. The result is positions can get too large, and we end up chasing losses and wasting our hard earned profits. Many a proprietary trader at an investment bank in the

City who may only deal 4 or 5 times a year will finish the year as the bank's top trader. Once again Warren Buffet sums up the situation perfectly: "Lethargy, bordering on sloth, is the cornerstone of an investment style... Much success can be attributed to inactivity".

If you are going to take on the market with any real degree of success you will need to use all the weapons available to you. The most potent weapon in the last three years has been the ability to go short. You will need to be comfortable shorting the market. If you only buy you are cutting yourself off from one the most efficient sources of revenue available to the private trader, especially in today's equity markets.

To understand the necessity of self discipline to combat fear and greed is one thing, putting it into practice is quite another. I believe trading on-line can help solve many of these problems. More and more Cantor Index clients are choosing to transact their business via our on-line dealing platform. Often when we call into a dealing room during a busy market, the noise can panic us into trading, rather like the squawk boxes I mentioned earlier, but using the internet could help you think and react more calmly. The internet gives the added value of anonymity; this saves any need for embarrassment when trading and will eliminate any doubts you may have that you are not always receiving neutral prices, which is a concern with customers of some spread betting companies. You can easily monitor the market and your positions with continuously published prices, receiving instant confirmations of your trades. Language becomes less relevant; an advantage if you are unsure of the correct terminology, or if English is not your first language.

Trading on line also ensures your privacy, as you cannot be overheard as you deal. If you don't fancy entering the ring yourself, send a computer in for you!

I hope I have managed to give you some useful pointers to enjoying successful trading. There are no shortcuts or easy solutions; in the main simple self-discipline is the key. But don't be too hard on yourself if that discipline slips once in a while. I know I have broken my own rules on more than a few occasions; indeed there isn't a trader who hasn't. We are only human and it is, after all, our common human qualities that make financial markets such a fascinating environment and what a boring place they would be if that were not so.

Lewis Findlay
Managing Director, Cantor Index

Securities Institute Publishing

Each publication provides a detailed overview and practical introduction to key topics within financial services.

Our range consists of re–worked and updated notes from our popular courses. These publications are a useful reference for everyone who needs to grasp the basics of a topic – fast!

To place an order or find out more, call now on *020 7645 0680*.

ADVANCED OPERATIONS MANAGEMENT

This book will suit personnel in financial and commodities based organisations and is useful for supervisors/junior managers in areas interacting with operations such as compliance, audit, technology, system/information suppliers, exchanges, clearing houses and custody providers. Contents include:

- The Management of Risk
- Securities Financing
- Treasury Operations
- Resource Management
- Utilising Technology
- Procedure Documentation
- Client Management

288pp paperback, ISBN: 1 84307 045 6, 1st edition

INTRODUCTION TO BOND MARKETS

Introduction to Bond Markets provides a comprehensive, authoritative description and analysis of the bond markets. The book considers basic 'plain vanilla' bonds and elementary bond mathematics, before looking at the array of different instruments available. Contents include:

- Bond Yield Measurement
- Corporate Debt Markets
- Eurobonds
- Risk Management
- Off–Balance Sheet Instruments
- Government Bond Markets
- Emerging Bond Markets.

410pp paperback, ISBN: 1 900520 79 6, 2nd edition

AN INTRODUCTION TO CORPORATE FINANCE
- Transactions and Techniques

Introduction to Corporate Finance provides readers with the key elements of corporate finance. The book introduces the principle techniques used in corporate finance, combined with practical experience and hands-on, numerically orientated case studies.

- Sources of Capital
- Flotations/Initial Public Offerings
- Mergers and Acquisitions
- Management Buy Outs
- Determining the Cost of Capital
- International Equity Offerings
- Valuing Securities

96pp paperback, ISBN: 1 900520 09 5, 1st edition

THE FUNDAMENTALS OF CREST

The Fundamentals of CREST gives a detailed overview of securities administration and settlement through the CREST system. It is illustrated throughout with diagrams and tables, bullet points and summaries.

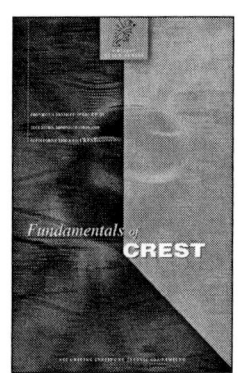

- Handling Certificated Securities
- Corporate Actions and Claims
- Stock Loans and Collateral.

128pp paperback, ISBN: 1 900520 98 2, 2nd edition

DICTIONARY OF FINANCIAL & SECURITIES TERMS

This updated and greatly expanded 2nd edition
gives definitions of frequently used terms in the
financial and securities industry. Also included is
a comprehensive listing of abbreviations,
acronyms and industry websites. Over 2,500
entries.

- What is BIFFEX?
- What does CDP stand for?
- What are the Conduct of Business Rules?
- What is the definition of Debt/Equity Ratio?

Included with the dictionary is a FREE
CD–ROM version for users to load onto their PC for easy reference at home
or at work.

400pp paperback, ISBN: 1 84307 023 5, 2nd edition

ECONOMIC & MONETARY UNION

Economic and Monetary Union (EMU) is the
system that links together the economies and
currencies of the participating European countries.
The European Central Bank has become
responsible for centralised monetary policy. What
does the Euro mean for you?

- Convergence
- Impact of the Euro on the markets
- Preparing for the future.

28pp paperback, ISBN: 1 900520 31 1, 1st edition

INTRODUCTION TO EQUITY MARKETS

Introduction to Equity Markets provides an overview of the current financial services industry. The book introduces the reader to different types of companies and shares as well as analysis of UK markets. An overview of dealing and settlement in some of the world's major markets is also featured. Contents include:

- Shareholders and Company Law
- Issuing Shares – The Primary Market
- Trading Shares – The Secondary Market
- Settlement of Transactions
- Major Overseas Exchanges and Indices
- Dividends, Bonus Issues and Rights Issues
- Company Accounts.

170pp paperback, ISBN: 1 84307 034 0, 2nd edition

AN INTRODUCTION TO FUND MANAGEMENT

Introduces readers to the economic rationale for the existence of funds, the different types available, investment strategies and other related issues from the perspective of the investment manager. Includes relevant formulae, equations and examples.

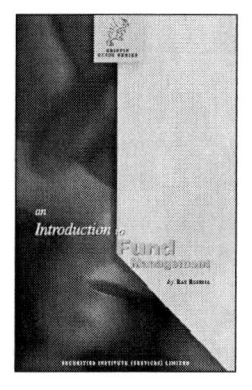

- Features and characteristics of funds
- Portfolio management and administration
- Performance measurement
- Investment mathematics.

160pp paperback, ISBN: 1 84307 022 7, 2nd edition

FUNDAMENTALS OF GLOBAL OPERATIONS MANAGEMENT

This book will help you to understand the role of operations terms and what is happening in the industry that impacts on operations. It is ideal for anyone new to or aspiring to become a supervisor or manager.Contents include:

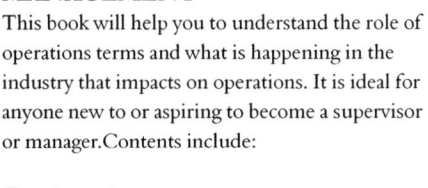

- Operations management
- Markets
- Banking, broking and institutional clients
- Concepts of risk
- Clearing and settlement
- Custody
- Technology
- Regulation and compliance

272pp paperback, ISBN: 1 84307 014 6, 1st edition

INTRODUCTION TO THE GILT STRIPS MARKET

Introduction to the Gilt Strips Market provides a thorough description and analysis of gilt strips. The contents describe and define strips as a financial instrument and examine the use and application of gilt strips within the context of the capital markets as a whole. Contents include:

- Zero–coupon bonds
- The yield curve
- Interest rate risk for strips
- Settlement, tax and regulatory issues
- Trading and strategy

192pp paperback, ISBN: 1 84307 006 5, 2nd edition

THE PREVENTION OF MONEY LAUNDERING

This quick guide looks at the scale of the problem and efforts taken to overcome it: an essential reference for all who are concerned to identify attempts at money laundering within their organisation.

- What is money laundering?
- Money laundering and the law
- How do you spot it in the process, and what to do.

48pp paperback, ISBN: 1 84307 005 7, 2nd edition

UNDERSTANDING REGULATION AND COMPLIANCE

Understanding Regulation & Compliance outlines the new regulatory structure in the post-N2 environment, introducing the areas regulated under the *Financial Services and Markets Act 2000*, the role of the *Financial Services Authority* and the rules imposed on firms. It also introduces other important regulatory areas such as *Insider Dealing and Money Laundering*. Topics include:

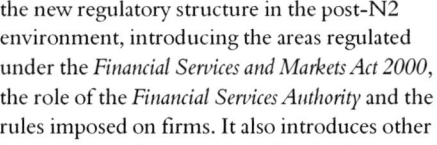

- Financial Services & Markets Act 2000
- Financial Services Authority
- FSA Handbook
- Control over individuals
- Conduct of business rules
- Client assets
- Improper dealings
- Money laundering

176pp paperback, ISBN: 1 84307 062 6, 3rd edition

INTRODUCTION TO REPO MARKETS

An Introduction to Repo Markets provides a comprehensive description and analysis of the repo markets. The text has been written to cater for those with little or no previous experience of the repo markets, though it also develops the subject matter to sufficient depth to be of use to more experienced practitioners. Contents include:

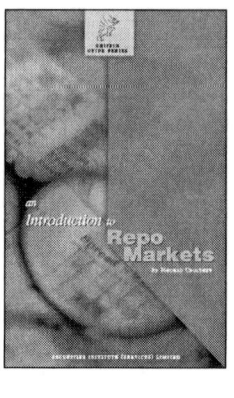

- Uses and economic functions of repo
- Accounting, Tax and Capital issues
- The UK gilt repo market
- The implied repo rate and basis trading
- Repo and the yield curve

240pp paperback, ISBN: 1 900520 86 9, 2nd edition

AN INTRODUCTION TO SWAPS

An Introduction to Swaps gives a detailed overview of how the various categories of swap work, how they are traded and what they are used for. Topics include interest rate swaps, managing risk, asset swaps, currency swaps. The book is illustrated with over 50 diagrams and tables.

- Managing risk with swaps
- Asset swaps
- Currency swaps.

160pp paperback, ISBN: 1 900520 21 4, 1st edition

AN INTRODUCTION TO VALUE–AT–RISK

An Introduction to Value–at–Risk has been written for those with little or no previous under-standing of or exposure to the concepts of risk management and Value–at–Risk. Topics include applications of VaR, instrument structures, stress testing, VaR for corporates, credit risk and legal/regulatory issues.

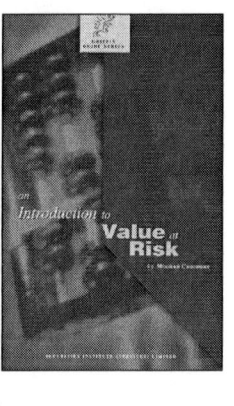

- Risk and Risk management
- VaR and Derivatives, Fixed Interest products.
- VaR for Corporates

208pp paperback, ISBN: 1 84307 035 9, 3rd edition

SECURITIES INSTITUTE PUBLISHING

For further details on these and other new titles, contact Customer Operations on 020 7645 0680

Forthcoming titles

Retail Publications

- Reports & Accounts Demystified
- An Introduction to Derivatives
- Prime Brokerage, Custody and Fund Administration
- Mutual Funds

Securities Institute/Butterworth-Heinemann Global Capital Markets Series

- IPO and Equity Offerings
- Controls, Procedures and Risk
- Clearing, Settlement and Custody
- Managing Technology in the Operations Function
- Relationship and Resource Management in Operations
- Understanding the Markets
- Credit Risk

For further information on this series please call *01865 888180* or visit http://www.bh.com/finance/

We plan to introduce new titles into our retail range in the forthcoming year. All the titles listed are provisional and may be subject to alteration.

124